Great Nana Sings

By

Patricia Hancock Rogers

Published in the United States of America

ISBN 978-1-956741-19-3 (SC)
ISBN 978-1-956741-46-9 (HC)

Spirit of Truth
222 West 6th Street
Suite 400, San Pedro, CA, 90731
www.stellarliterary.com

Order Information and Rights Permission:

Quantity sales. Special discounts might be available on quantity purchases by corporations, associations, and others. For details, contact the publisher at the address above.

For Book Rights Adaptation and other Rights Permission. Call us at toll-free 1-888-945-8513 or send us an email at admin@stellarliterary.com.

Dedication

I dedicate this book to all my children, grands, and great grands. And to my friends who encouraged me to tell my story. Those who trusted me to lead them and direct them in Classical Productions.

Introduction

My DNA is the personification of me. In the early 1600s in America, my ancestors arrived on different ships from different lands. More incredible is from the Motherland, Africa two parts, 50% Nigerian and 6% Kenyan. All other ancestors came from13% Iberian, 7% United Kingdom,13% Sierra Leonean, West Asian, Massai, South Asian, and Ashkenazi Jewish. What a mixture. No wonder I wanted to visit the world. Heaven knows that is probably for my free mind thinking. I never felt anyone better than me. I have an affinity for all folks and try not to notice differences. I believe people are more alike than they think.

When I began to travel around the world, I never felt frightened or alone; even with the company I traveled with, I toured most of the time on my own. People smiled and talked with me, and they respected me. I want to visit a few places, but I'm not in a rush. I wonder how I have so many ancestors from so many places in the world? I guess they too liked to travel, and life just goes around.

Contents

Chapter 1

History In A Nutshell

How the Hancock's Got Their Name

Abraham Lincoln signed the Emancipation Proclamation, President of the US in September 1862 was put on record in January 1863. As soon as word got out, the slaves packed their wagons with family and goods and migrated from the plantation in Virginia, the name of Hancock and Jackson. My great paternal grandfather chose the name Hancock. They migrated to West Virginia. When my paternal grandfather was born a free man, he grew a property owner in St. Albans, West Virginia. I loved granddaddy. He would visit our house and sit on the front porch in the swing; then, he would show me his gold pocket watch tucked in the small pocket of his vest in his three-piece gray flannel business suit. He also wore a derby hat. He would ask me what I wanted for Christmas, saying "plates" I wanted a tea set with plates. He was a medium-tall sophisticated brown skin man. When he died, he left the property, but no one claimed it? I was a teenager when I heard about it and had no idea what they were saying. Most of our family is unaware of our history, so I will share thoughts that come to me now and then.

My father had a brother John and a sister Helen. My mother was the thirteenth child in her family. My maternal grandfather was a coal miner in Raleigh, West Virginia. My grandmother was a Baptist socialite. She had a white seamstress make her dresses for her Baptist conventions. My mother was spoiled, and her older sister Stella took care of her buying her the best dresses. We still have some of her China and glassware kept in her China closet. In other words, these Negro people were living free and enjoying it.

When the slaves on my maternal family left the plantation, they settled in another part of Virginia, Louisiana County. I visited some years ago and was informed that the Whites were offering very little money to sell their land. To this day, I don't know how it all turned out. I saw my great-great-grandparent's home all covered with overgrown vegetation, they were having a family reunion, and a giant caterpillar machine was next to the old house. I imagine tearing it down the next day. The ancestors' graves were in the church's yard, and I took pictures of those I will never know. They were the Prices.

My mother's mother and her husband, James Lindsay, migrated from Virginia to West Virginia. My father's people also migrated to West Virginia. They prospered as coal miners, men's jobs, and the women were all homemakers. Years later, my mother's family moved to the capital, Charleston. They lived well and prospered.

Chapter 2
The Founding Fore Fathers and Mothers

We have not given the founding fore Mother her just dues. She was snatched from her land along with her children from Mother Africa, still being bred on ships for the pleasure of her Capturers. Arriving in the new world, landed on the blocks of slavery markets, known as a good breeder, for the sake of the to-be owners, to start the foundation of the nation.

The warmth of her nurturing breastfeeding the young of her owner and her own. Pushing aside her own bred by her countryman to give her all to the master's child. She produced enough labor for the plantations, the mansions, the fields with laborers to keep family and housework perfect. In contrast, others picked, farmed, and cultivated the land for building towns and cities.

How shall we celebrate and give praise to her as they do for the Fore Fathers? Unveil her true identity, tell the truth about the founding of this country.

Patricia Hancock Rogers - 2017

Chapter 3
My Father
Charles Edward Hancock

My father was born in January 1906. All his children loved him except my younger brother Louie. Louie was born when my father was away at the state hospital, so he never knew him.

He worked for the Diamond Ice @ Coal company, he delivered ice to the homes every morning, as you know, 1930's most homes were using iceboxes because refrigerators were not invented at least for the market yet. He was rather tall and had very elegant-looking red hair and light skin color.

When I was about 4 four years old, World War 2 was calling men to draft for the army. My father worried every day as he read the newspapers after work. He always said., "I do not want to go to war because who would take care of my children? He sat on the front porch reading the Daily mail newspaper as my younger brother Billy, and I watched through the screen door. One day, the job secretary was passing after work, and my father went out the gate to show her the news headlines of the war escalating. A white man coming down the street interfered and said my father was annoying the woman, so he called the police, and they came and handcuffed my father and took him away while my brother Billy and I watched. Daddy said to the police, let me go in to tell my wife. We ran to the kitchen to tell her that the police had taken daddy away. She stood frozen and very pregnant with her eighth baby. Of course, they did not allow him to say goodbye to my mother and swept him away. For four years, my father was away. At one time, he tried to run away to come home. He was caught and returned to the institution, starved and beaten to death.

I know it because I was with Aunt Stella, who went to the funeral home as Mrs. Harding, the funeral home director, told her the grim story. She said he was skin and bones from starvation, and his nails were ghostly long and beaten badly.

This is my Fathers' Day tribute, and I needed to tell my family, these days are still taking young Black Fathers away from their wives and children. Daddy was thirty-nine years old when he left us and was forty-three when he left the world.

This Is A letter to All My Family. May God Bless You All, and Do Not forget to Bless Your Father.

June 16, 2020

Chapter 4

My Mother and Father

I remember both parents at an early age. Mother was feeding me. My dad took me from her and said, "Give me my baby girl. My mother took me back and said, "Give me my baby girl. I believe that early knowledge of love from both parents instilled a confidence in me that will be with me forever.

Mom was a soft-spoken, gentle, and diligent worker. Early in their marriage, she told us, that my father went to the railroad tracks to look for coal or pieces of wood to burn in the fireplace, he was arrested by the police. My father was sent to work for the WPA, a federal department project set up by President Franklin D. Roosevelt for public works during the depression. When the general building was completed, my father went to work for the Diamond Ice & Coal company. Well-liked by his boss Mr. Capito, owner of the company. He would drive him places he needed to go, especially to the golf course. He even gave him a golf bag with clubs that my brother Billy and I would often examine and smell the brown leather bag. My father also chewed apple tobacco and, at times, smoked a pipe. They were a happy couple. He would get up early in the morning and have his cup of coffee, then throw his leather pad over his shoulder to protect his shoulder from the ice hooks that he threw over the pad.

He would tuck his ice pick in a special belt, and these were the tools of the iceman.

He was rather popular at the Baptist picnics in the summer; we have a picture of him quite handsome with his straw hat of the 1930s. He had a unique wardrobe with drawers for his shirts and personal items. It also had a closet for his suits and a unique tie hanger. We examined everything. Everyone called him Charlie. He was well-liked in the community. He always bragged about his family.

My mother baked biscuits, cornbread, and hot rolls on holidays. She would churn butter and make vanilla ice cream on Sundays in the summer. We were happy children. There were chickens in the back yard, and many times, Hobos would hop off the trains, come to our house, knock on the door, and ask for food. She would tell us to tell them to go to the backdoor, and she would fry them an egg sandwich. We had a large backyard and played in it most of the time. Daddy put lily ponds in the front yard, and we would see in the springtime tadpoles and frogs.

Our neighborhood was diverse. There was hillbilly's next door to us, and on the other side were two African American sisters Ms. Price and Mrs. Moore. Mrs. Moore was the pianist at the Baptist church. Ms. Price favored my oldest sister Mary Julia. Across the street was an Italian family, two girls one my age and one my younger sister Nancy's age. Next door to them was a Greek family.

When daddy died, my mother received $10,000 from the WPA, insurance police earned by the workers. Mr. Capito offered the house to us, but she did not want it because she would have had to move it, and it was not worth it. We stayed with Aunt Stella one year and moved into the Washington Manor, a government housing for middle-income families.

We began a new life singing as a family, my brother Louie was a

genius at the piano, and we had a career singing concerts every Sunday and many times throughout the week. It was six of us, my elder brothers were in the army, and when they came home, they immediately got married. The singing kept me happy, and we were busy.

Father and Mother

Chapter 5

My Life

Where do I start? Well, we all know when and where we were born, at least most of us do. On December 6, 1937, I was born at 209 Welch Street, Charleston, West Virginia. Around six o'clock in the morning.

I was told that my dad ran out of the house to tell the neighbors to come to see his redhead, baby girl. Nurse Mc Millan was my nurse, the city provided nurse service to help deliver at-home births. My aunt Stella was there, of course, as always, she cared for my mother since she was a baby, they were years apart. Welch street was on the east side of Charleston, and Aunt Stella lived on the west side of town, the middle-class folks. Mother said I said my first word at six months old. I am still at it quite fervently.

Aunt Stella decided I should be her buddy. She would take me to her home to stay with her more than my other siblings. She would tell my mother that she was going to New York and buy me a new wardrobe. I always felt like a poor little rich girl. Hanging with her taught me about women's problems, mainly because she owned an automobile and drove all over to visit friends, and they would shed their woes about their husbands. What is a divorce, I wondered? Everyone smoked except Aunt Stella. People thought she was our grandmother. She was my mother's watch over my older sister.

When I was two years old, I learned to sing songs I heard on the radio. One day, my mother was in bed with a new bay and called out to find who that singing was? My older sister Mary said that's Pat singing. Well, it was on, my sisters Mary Julia and Frances Dee thought we should sing like the Andrew sisters, a famous Italian sister singing group. Aunt Stella heard us and immediately became our agent. Her neighbor, the White family, was Seventh Day Adventist and their youngest daughter was a genius at the piano. She decided that we would sing at their church. I was now five years old. We did, and that started my lifelong career in the world of music. Aunt Stella took me to Dr. Maude Wanzer Lane to take piano lessons. Ms. Lane would listen from her kitchen and know that I was using the wrong finger and missing notes. Dr. Lane was our high school band director and music teacher's high school. She died at an early age. I attended Boyd elementary and junior high school. My fourth-grade sister Mary thought we should be in the high school talent show. We did but as solo acts. I won the first prize; Mary won the second and Frances won the third. Until my senior year in high school, I would win the first prize. In my senior year, the teachers in charge asked me if I would be the guest artist for someone else to have a chance.

I took my brother Louis to piano lessons with Mr. John. I also took classes and advanced nicely; however, Louie was a genius and could play anything he heard. We had a family group and called our group the Hancock singers. We sang all types of music, according to what the program affair might be. We performed for church concerts, PTA's, meetings, any organization we were prepared to sing the music necessary for the event. I was fortunate to have highly trained music teachers from first grade, Mrs. Maude Clark, third grade Katheryn Ferguson through junior high school, and Mrs. India Harris. We sang classical, Negro spirituals, Broadway selections.

When I was thirteen, I went to New York with Aunt Stella and tied first place at the Apollo theater singing Dinah Washington's Good Daddy Blues. I met Ms. Washington when she came to Charleston when I was eleven years old. She played the piano for me; I always sang her songs for talent shows, and I was called little Dinah. She gave me an eight by ten photograph signed "to Pat, I love you because you love me." Then there was the Jabberwock at West Virginia State College in Institute, WV.

It was a Black and White ball named by my voice teacher, I later learned thirty years later. I was the guest performing artist for the evening. The AKA sorority presented our high school Debutants ball in the spring before graduation. I was invited to participate and was overjoyed. In the chapter on the twice a debutant, I have described the Deb ball in the chapter.

A brownie scout troop in a Tom Thumb Wedding

Sisters

Frances, Mary Julia, and Patricia

Hancock Singers

Chapter 6

I Was Born To Sing

When I was six months old, my mother said, I said my first word. At two years old, I remember singing on the radio; my mother heard the song and asked who is that singing. My older sister Mary said it was Pat; I was singing," When You Were Sweet Sixteen" I believe it was Judy Garland on the radio. My older sister Mary put together my sister Frances who was older than me, and me together as a trio. We would imitate the Andrew Sisters on the radio. One day my aunt Stella heard us and bought us a gospel songbook, and we started singing sacred songs. My first time on the public stage was at five years old. We were singing at the Seventh Day Adventist church. Aunt Stella got her neighbor across the street from her to play the piano for us, Elmire White. She was a genius and spoiled me forever for a good pianist. One day, my younger brother Louis walked to the piano and started to play by ear. When he developed the technic of accompanying, we had a family group, the Hancock singers.

We grew and became very popular, concertizing every Sunday. My first singing solo was at Boyd elementary school in the second grade for the school assembly; I sang My Country Tis of Thee. When the high school started their talent shows, Sister Mary came home from school telling Momma she was going to sing. the Frances said she too was going to sing a solo, my cousin Helen said, what about Pat, I was nine years old, they agreed I should sing. They chose, The Masquerade is Over by Little Jimmy Scott. I sang and won the first prize; Mary won the second prize. That was the beginning of my popular singing and many years of first prize winnings. When I was 13, Aunt Stella took me to New York to sing on the stage of the famous Apollo theater. I tied the first place, singing Good Daddy Blues by Dinah Washington, whom I met when she came to my hometown, and she played the piano for me when I sang "I Want to Cry When I Hear Your Name." She gave me an 8x10 photo autographed, "I Love you Because You Love Me." Maybe I did. All I know is that her songs were chosen by my cousin Helen Washington.

One Sunday afternoon, we were on a show with Mahalia Jackson and Della Reese. Della said to me, "don't ruin your voice singing the gospel music; 30 years later, I was in California with the New York City Opera company, I visited the Christal Cathedral, and she was the guest soloist, I met the pastor, Robert Schuller and told him what she had said to me; he called down to catch her, but we just missed her Limo it was going through the gate.

I was offered two college scholarships at the age of 13 at the Tawawa School of religion at Wilberforce U, provided to me by Bishop A.J. Allen; at my high school graduation. Our keynote speaker, a minister from Philadelphia, offered to give me a scholarship to Temple U in Philadelphia. I thanked him but chose Wilberforce in Ohio. I attended Wilberforce one year, the Bishop died that summer, and I had no money of my own. I met my husband William Rogers at Wilberforce. We both were in the college choir, and his father could no longer pay his bill, so we decided two could live as cheap as one and get married that fall. We moved to Cincinnati, Ohio. Out of the marriage were five children. The first were twin girls. Then a son and the last two were girls. Eight years in Cincinnati, I moved with the children to Brooklyn, NY, with my mother.

After a near-death experience, I found a voice teacher, Lola Wilson Hayes, an African American teacher who did not look it. I lived on 5th Avenue in the same building as the Infamous Marion Anderson. He lived in the penthouse of the building. She prepared me for my first union job, "the Broadway Extravaganza, directed by impresario Clyde Turner also, an African American tenor, we toured the United States. I was Maria from the West Side Story and a daughter from Fiddler on the Roof. Some years later, Bill passed away, and I raised the children on my own, making sure they all went to college. When my youngest daughter graduated, I returned to college and received a Master of Arts degree. I was informed that I had earned an MS degree as well. I was working on my doctoral at Columbia Teachers College in New York, I decided not to borrow more money and would have completed it in the following spring. I regret today that I did not follow the course.

Meanwhile, I was already a member of the Metropolitan Opera associate chorus and a member of the New York City opera associate chorus. Juggling operas from both houses, and the opera Treemonisha at Kennedy Center on Broadway. I spent 34 years at Lincoln Center. New York City Opera was the longest stay. Porgy and Bess was my last opera at the Met, 1985, and again in 1991. I worked for many opera companies in the New York area. My world travels were with the Virginia opera company to South America and the Living Arts Company to Japan, the United Kingdom, Taiwan, Australia, New Zealand, performing the opera Porgy & Bess. I also was a Delaware Artist in Residence; I was living there and was a substitute teacher in the public school system when I was not touring. In 1978 I toured the cross country with the Voices Incorporated, out of Harlem, NY as an artist in residence performing and teaching Black History. One of the most fulfilling times of my life. In 2002, I won the Ms. Delaware pageant for the senior Ms. America contest. The NYC opera company performed at Kennedy Center in Washington every year before its opera company. I loved going to DC; NYC opera also performed at Wolf trap in Virginia in the spring for several years.

The off-season for the opera allowed me to study abroad. I went to Blonay, Switzerland, to study French art songs, and Austria to study German lieder the following year. The newspaper said, "She appeared in magical radiance." I was preparing for my New York debut at the Carnegie Recital Hall. Raoul Abdul of the Amsterdam news hailed my concert as a Voice of Beauty.

Some years later, I wanted to form my own company of singers. I was encouraged by a young white man I was sitting by, on my way to Kennedy center, with NYC opera company, who said to me," why don't you all get your own company?" I did not get angry; I got even. I formed Classical productions with singers I met at the two remarkably diverse groups. That's because I am a pretty eclectic person who likes people. NYSCA funded us for around 20 years. I loved those singers. We performed for almost empty houses and wonderful ballroom spaces, celebrating our many anniversaries. I made costumes in the early years and gowns to look like the singers. We wore pearl earrings and necklaces that I bought to be uniform. The men wore red ties and cummerbunds, which I also supplied so that they would look harmonious together. One of my favorite concert venues was in Brooklyn, on the pier on the Music Barge. Our Christmas show was exceptional; the barge on the east river had a fireplace decorated with holiday trimmings that gave way to singing holiday songs and always an excellent reception afterward. People always remembered and would ask us when were we having another barge concert? Our group would constantly change singers but were replaced with the same caliber or better than before.

I thought I wanted an assistant at one time, and I hired a gentleman to assist me. He combined Classical Productions with the Julliard Jazz band, performing Duke Ellington's best. He then tried to change our name and steal the group from me. Well, he had another thought coming, I saw the real tiger in me rise, and he scampered. We performed in Washington, DC, for the Ms. DC Pageant for several years. My dear friend sponsored the pageant every year following her crowning of Ms. DC in 2002. We met in Charleston, SC, when we participated in the senior women's Ms. America pageant's national pageant. I was the queen of Delaware; and Charleston, West Virginia, for my acceptance for the WV Hall of Fame 2008. One year we traveled to Austria to sing with the Harlem singers in a Porgy & Bess concert. My male singers were dominant in the male section. Every spring for many years, we performed at the United Nations. Our first performance earned us a United Nations Medal of Honor. For thirteen years, we had a standing spring concert for the Marble Collegiate Church's Wednesday afternoon concert hour.We performed 42 years ago, and the Covid-19 pandemic stopped all the public performances. I look forward to serving with four senior artists who have been successful in their art forms. This program will be performed on August 6 and 7, 2021.

Chapter 7

A Young Girl Growing Up

I remember being a happy child most of the time. I had siblings who were constantly engaged in some activity, playing, working, and rehearsing together. We even had to sleep two together because we had such a large family. There were four boys and four girls.

I seemed to be able to see in the future as a child. For example, when Billy and I listened to the Santa Clause on the radio, I told him that we would see him right where the dial was one day. I would tell my younger siblings that Santa was on the roof, bringing us toys. They believed me; actually, I thought it myself. We did not get many toys, usually one apiece., but we were just as happy as we had been given a lot. My aunt Stella would take us to her house, and there was a toy box full of toys and books to read and my favorite book, it had a xylophone in it to play as you sang. These were toys my cousin had as a child. Many years later, when I was a guide at the Lyndhurst castle, her toys were many more and some even better than the Gould children.

When my mother had to kill the chickens and clean them, I told Billy that we would buy chickens already cut up and packaged one day. When I was older, I dreamed I was singing in the college choir. I was standing in the middle right in front of the conductor, well I have a picture of the Wilberforce choir, and there I am standing right in the middle in front of the conductor. I dreamed I was in New York going to a voice teachers' apartment on the fifth avenue as an adult. I went into the building, and I came to an elevator. I sensed that Marion Anderson was there; years later, when I moved to New York, I was given the address to my voice teacher's residence, and as I turned the corner onto the fifth avenue, I knew I had been to the building before, in a dream. Marion Anderson lived in the penthouse of the building.

My Aunt Stella was our wardrobe mistress for the girls because she liked shopping. My mother was always busy with a new baby and did not have time to do the shopping, and when she went to the grocery store, Aunt Stella would drive her. It was a good thing because the number of groceries was a lot.

During World War two, the people were given rationing stamps to shop with, according to the size of the family. My mother had quite a lot, and neighbors often asked if she could spare some. They had small families, and Momma would always share what she had. I remember at one time. She bought 50 pounds of flour two 25lb sacks. She learned that it was challenging to keep flour because it could mildew as the second bag did. Aunt Stella would take us to her house on the weekends many times. We would get our Saturday night bath; she would shampoo the girl's hair straighten, and curl our hair. The boys my younger two brothers, the older boys were grown up. She would send Billy and Louie to the barber next door for their haircuts.

I was a brownie scout and loved going to summer camp. One summer, about eleven years, we went camping, and one of the scout troops put together an exciting African dance with the beat of drums. I came home, got together the neighborhood kids, and taught them the danced added other singing songs to fill out the program. One of the girls, my friend Sissy Whitlow, suggested we have the show in the recreation room of the complex where we lived. I went to the office and got permission to use the space. We made posters and invited the whole complex; a crowd came, paying 10 cents. Afterward, we served Kool-aid and cookies. This was my first show production. Today I have had forty years of directing and producing, Classical Productions.

Aunt Stell that was her nickname in short that we called her made some of our dresses and often bought them ready-made, and she would make her changes; for example, the broomstick skirt was popular, an oversized ruffle at the hem of the skirt, the big girls got them, but Nancy and I were too young yet. She always dressed us alike. I wouldn't say I liked it; I wanted my style and no one else like mine. I am still that way; I like being different. We had black patent leather shoes and white anklet socks for dress-up, sturdy oxford, usually brown shoes for school; one year, I got oxblood-colored oxfords no one else would even dare to wear them, but I liked them. The jumpers, blouses, and skirts with a warm sweater were the fashion of the day.

When I was about ten years old, I was at the Baby shop with a momma who was buying a suit for my nephew. An exclusive Quarrier Street shop catered from babies to young girls. I saw a dress with a gold quilted bottom skirt and a black velvet top with rhinestone buttons. I asked her to buy me the dress, it was expensive 25.00, but she loved the good quality and did not mind buying it. Remember, I was the lead singer in the family, and that had its merit. A year later, I was browsing the Baby shop and saw a beautiful maroon velvet dress with taffeta ribbon trim ruffle around the lower skirt and a layer of bustle ruffles down the back. It was to beg for.

Again, the singer got what she asked for. Momma was stringent; we were not privileged to socialize with other children unless it was the members of the church and church activities. Parents in those days judged you by the company you kept. Once as we got older, I bravely told her that we wanted to attend the football game with our friends, and surprisingly she said yes. I had learned to negotiate like a diplomat. I used the same skill with classmates when I asked them to vote for me to be the queen of my class. The royal blood was initiated in me from that day on. The class queens rode in the parade on top of convertible cars for the football homecoming game. We were dressed beautifully. My girlfriend Yvonne Jackson was the queen of our high school, Miss Garnet high" I did not mind being in the royal court that beautiful Saturday. Garnet was an outstanding school. It measured up to any school in America, I believed. It proved to be so; the doctors, lawyers, teachers, government officials, etc., came when we had our high school reunion, they showed off. Years later, Yvonne and I would meet again in Brooklyn, NY, living on the same street a block from each other.

Momma shopped at Franken Berger's men's department store for my brothers. It was the finest men's store in town. She bought our dining room set, pieces we still have, from Woodrum's fine furniture department store. She bought beautiful fabric for chair covers and made living room couch and armchair covers trimmed with silk braided fringe.

Years later, when we drove from New York to Charleston for our high school reunion, we would stop at the Greenbrier Hotel, a national treasure, for the incredibly famous president and other national figures. At one time, this hotel was for the president of the United States to take cover underground if there was an invasion in the country. The hotel's decor was magnificent. Ironically, the chair covers were like my mother's same fabric and patterns for our living room. Every four years, when we went to our high school reunion, we would take a break at the Greenbrier, making sure to arrive about three for high tea. The grounds were beautiful, and through the years, the wealthy would spend the summer for the sulfur baths and other activities. Aunt Stells' husband's family were cooks, and some were cooks at the Greenbrier hotel. Aunt Stells' husband, Ulysses, was a restaurant owner in the heart of downtown Charleston, on Summers Street.

Downtown Charleston, right in the heart of town, were the black business owners, the Ferguson hotel, the Ferguson theater, the barbershop, and our high school, Garnet. The First Baptist Church and the Simpson Methodist Church. The Preston funeral Home was two blocks from Capitol Street. The old Harden's Funeral home was across the street from Woodrum's fine furniture Department store, where Momma bought her dining room set and the fabric to make her chair covers. One year she sent me to Woodrum's for the new style of crisscross curtains. Our apartment at the Washington Manor was pretty and comfortable. When Christmas came, we would wait until late Christmas Eve to buy our trees because they would be half price. Our house was charming on Christmas.

I became the hairdresser for family and friends in high school. I learned how to dress hair from Aunt Stella, who kept our hair dressed. She made Shirley temple curls, and I had bangs. Sometimes we would go to Mrs. Harvey's house to get our hair done. She had an amputee's leg and walked with crutches. One of her daughters, Beverly, went to Howard University in Washington DC, and she came home speaking French. I admired her so, although I knew she was showing off, it made me see that I would go to college.

Growing up in Charleston, I was pretty busy, constantly rehearsing for the girl's ensemble, the glee club, the church choir, the family group, preparing for the annual talent shows, practicing the piano, and taking my little brother Louie to piano lessons. Louie only needed to hear the music, and he could play by ear. He was quite a genius. He became one of the finest pianists I knew in all my life.

Chapter 8

A Debutant Twice

In my senior year in high school, the AKA sorority of West Virginia State College presented a debutante ball; they sent invitations to chosen young ladies in our senior class; I received one, and of course, I accepted the invite. I was a wallflower at the school dances but always dreamed of dancing with the best male dancer in the school. That person just happened to be Hercules Woods. Some teachers thought he was not in the upper society; however, he was a church member, and I thought he was perfect. We danced perfectly beautifully the evening of the ball.

In September, I hurried off to Wilberforce College. I was met at the Greyhound bus stop by a young senior ministry student. Many years later, he became a bishop of the AME church. He claimed me to be his girl after meeting me; they called him" Preach," at the time, I was not interested in anyone. I arrived with $50.00 my mother gave me and was on a scholarship paid by the Bishop, A.J. Allen. One of the Fraternity organizations decided to have a debutantes' ball. I was invited to participate but, I told them I was already a debutant; they would not have it so, I became a debutant twice. I wore the same gown my cousin, Helen, bought me for the first ball. I was given gifts for my whole wardrobe by friends and admirers who wanted to provide me with graduation gifts. I was a blessed young lady. I became the soprano soloist of the college choir. I was told the freshmen did not travel with the choir, but my voice was an exception, and since I had solo roles, I would have to travel with the choir. We traveled to Detroit, Michigan, to perform Handel's Messiah. I was the soprano soloist, and William Rogers was the tenor Soloist; the choirmaster gave me the job of teaching Bill the role. He had a perfect tenor sound and constantly informed me of it because his high school choir master told him so. We returned home for the Christmas holidays, and Bill wrote me a letter saying he missed me, and his mother said he was in love.

We returned to school for spring term, went to the movies, and got on with our separate studies, he was a premed student, and I was a music major. Bill was an A student; I, on the other hand, was a B student. Wilberforce was celebrating their centennial year. The choir was given the task of presenting a musical play written by an alumni gentleman. I was the leading lady; the choir was the chorus, the choir hardly rehearsed and depended on me to lead them. I was so overwhelmed by it that I forgot my part, and the play fell apart. The next day was the commencement, and I was to sing Michael's aria from the Opera Carmen, but the choirmaster thought I would not be able to do it. I think I had a breakdown. The school was out for the summer, and I got a ride home with my godfather, Rev. Ricks, who also inferred I was in love. I was working in Columbus, Ohio, at a grocery store when I received a letter that bishop A.J. Allen had passed away and that I no longer had a scholarship. Bill was working in Cincinnati, Ohio when his father informed him that he would not be able to pay for his school term in the fall. We discussed the idea that "two could live as cheap as one."

In the fall, October 13, 1957, we were married by my godfather Rev. Ricks at my home, and we had a reception at my Aunt Stella's house across the street from our house. After the wedding, we moved to Cincinnati, where Bill already had a job.

"Four Beauties", Debutantes, The Charleston Gazett
Barbara Denson, Patricia Hancock, Miss Hamblim,
Yvonne Jackson. 1955

Chapter 9

At Wilberforce

I decided to accept an offer to go to Wilberforce by bishop AJ Allen, who paid for my scholarship, but before returning for my sophomore year, the bishop died that summer. I loved Wilberforce. It is away from home, of all the restrictions at home. I thought I was a grown person at last.

I was highly active in the college choir, and the choir director depended on me to help teach other singers mainly, Bill Rogers, who was a tenor and had to learn the tenor soloist of the Handel's Messiah. We were preparing to go to Detroit, Michigan, to perform the works. I was the soprano soloist. The choir was highly accomplished in the repertoire, great anthems, and beautiful classical. Melvin Campbell was our organist; he was a genius. We toured many cities, and in New York, we were on a TV show," Strike it Rich," and won the $500.00 prize. I was window-shopping in New York while we were there and saw the popular poodle skirt and just had to have it.

I talked Bill into buying it for me. It seemed at the time he always had extra money. In another chapter, I was the leading lady in the centennial show in the spring for the alumni celebration. I was overworked learning the music and having to lead the choir. I was overcome with pressure and forgot the music. The show was a flop. I was very embarrassed but could not help it. The following was the commencement, and I was to sing Michaela's Aria from the opera Carmen, but the director thought it best I shouldn't sing. I was relieved because I thought I might forget the French lyrics. I had prepared the aria with the French Professor, Mrs. Ingersoll. I sang for her wedding that past December. I had to go to Ohio for her wedding and spend the night after the wedding. I was uncomfortable because I was alone and did not know anyone but her.

I did not know how much people thought of me until sixty years later when I was looking through the yearbook of 1955/1956. I read the comments many of the seniors said about me. One comment was, I hope Pat Hancock will stay four years like Shirley Barnes, well I did not. However, I made a career later in my life, and I never heard that she ever sings at Lincoln Center as I did for 34 years. Another senior said she hoped Pat Hancock would cultivate her speaking voice when she can't sing to become a speaker. Wow, how they got it right. I did not finish Wilberforce, but I received my MA and MS degrees from Columbia University Teachers College for twenty years. I have traveled around the world singing and could never dream of the places, countries, and cities I have enjoyed. I have presented my life story talking about my life experiences.

I believe Wilberforce has not received the honor it should have because it is the oldest Black College in the US and the first sit in the five and ten cent stores in Xenia, oh, no one remembers, I witnessed it, the NAACP group did so when I was a freshman at Wilberforce, the year 1955.

The report we get when they are preparing for voting is, "the educated white women of the suburbs, well we have had educated blacks since 1856, of course, they were not voting yet. However, African Americans have been going to Black Colleges since 1856, Wilberforce University the oldest. I spent only a year there, but it seemed a lifetime experience. I loved it, and the other schools I graduated from did not fulfill me as that wonderful year at Wilberforce.

My oldest twin daughter Neena graduated from Wilberforce and appreciated her one year there. She earned a degree in Art but worked for a Wall Street company. My granddaughter, Chrystal, spent four years there and graduated with a degree in business. She is an accountant for the state of New York.

When you send your children off to college, you don't expect the problems they will encounter for the sake of education. I have been to so many graduations with tucked-in pride I just never wanted to have a fall from pride, so I tried to be humble for it all. I have had children and grand grants to attend six Black colleges. Morehouse, my grandson Billy, Spellman, Gwendolyn, my son's children, Gary graduated Howard, my granddaughter Tamela, and I graduated from Bethune Cookman. She is an English teacher with two children also at Bethune. Her daughter Destiny is a senior, her son, Maleek, is a sophomore. My daughter Connie's son, my grandson Brian, attended Bethune but said he did not want a college bill. Christian, my son's youngest son, graduated from Morgan State, my granddaughter Kameko attended Florida AM a year, her brother Julian attended Lincoln U one year, graduated Temple U, they are my youngest daughter Candace's children, her youngest son Jared is a junior student at Bowie State.

Garnet High School Girls Ensemble

Wilberforce University Choir 1955 – 1956

Chapter 10

Marriage In Cincinnati

We lived in a lovely white-painted home on the second floor. Our landlady had a son, and we were the only tenants. She was the first African American on a beautiful tree-lined street in the neighborhood. Bill was working at the hospital, work he liked. He was a pre-med student. I was home expecting our first baby girl, how did I know it was a girl in those days?

Well, our doctor of color listened to the heartbeat and said girl babies have a faster heartbeat than boys. For sure, he was right. The only mistake was it was two instead of one. Patricia Neena and Pamela Teena. Bill and I made cribs out of orange crates. The nurse showed us how to pad and build them up. We moved from the small apartment to a larger one on Glenwood Avenue. Also, a neighborhood was integrated. My neighbors in the building had children, and we became friends. We moved in the winter and the spring when I bought the three babies out to take a walk; everyone was surprised to see that babies lived in our apartment because they never cried or made noise. It is true my babies were very contented and mainly were pleasant. My neighbor on the third floor made hot roles every day. The smell of the yeast baking drove me to find out how to make them. Then my next-door neighbor Mrs. Fields learned from me. We were constantly keeping up with each other. The third-floor neighbor made her little girls' dresses, so Mrs. Field and I had to do the same. Mrs. Field was a retired

Army nurse, she could polish her little girl's white high-top shoes expertly, so I had to learn how to polish Neena and Teena's white shoes. My son Gary was born when I lived at Glenwood Avenue. My doctor lived a few blocks from our house. He would stop by at night to see how I was doing; he could not deliver him because he was not a resident doctor at the Cincinnati general hospital. Dr. Brown was a young African American doctor exceedingly kind and caring.

Before Gary was born, I joined the Cincinnati May Festival chorus, I thought I could perform pregnant for the spring concert, but the baby decided to come the week. There were many children in the large apartment house, so I decided to move across the street with no children. The building owner said he did not rent to people with children, but I convinced him that my children were exceptional, and he allowed me to move in. One day, Bill bought a dog home, but he put his foot down when the building owner saw it. I let the children but no dogs. It was alright with me; I did not want to take care of a dog anyway; we had another baby girl, Connie. I told my husband I did not want any more children. His reply to me was, "you don't sound like a woman." He was busy with a very lucrative job for the next few months. He was captain of the bellhops at the new Carrousel Motel; after baby number five was born, Candy. I took all five walkings, we did not live far from the hospital where the new birth control clinic was located, we visited the clinic, and I did not have another baby.

One day he took the whole family to the auto dealer asked us to get out of the car and put us in a brand-new Mercury. We were doing very well financially. I was walking the children, and on the main road I saw our car go by, it was not him driving when he came home, I asked him about it, and he dismissed my argument that no one should be driving our car. A few days later, he came home disturbed, that same person had driven our car again and this time demolished it. Bill had not paid the insurance, and we had a total loss. He also chauffeured his boss's car and took him to Kentucky. On his way home, he hit a newspaper boy on a bike. We were sued for $50.000. This was quite a blow, so going on against him made it difficult to deal with. I, of course, replied, "we could pray for courage," and he said his god was the almighty dollar. I felt discouraged, and everything seemed to go downhill after that. I always knew that to pray would help. My mother taught me. Bill did not have the same family background that I had. We were in the church all the time, and at home, we prayed together every night and at every dinner setting. I knew that pray changed things. Bill was captain of the bellhops at the first million-dollar motel, the Carrousel Inn. It is a dump today. We stayed at the Motel when I was on tour with the Porgy and Bess company. It was gruesome compared to the one I knew in 1958.

Our marriage began to wane after a car accident. I was pregnant again with the baby girl, Candace. It was not a happy time for me, but I always tried to be the best mother I could be.

We moved again to a house not far from the hospital. One morning he went to work, and I dressed the babies, and we took a walk to the hospital to the new birth control clinic I heard about. The doctor asked if I would like to try the latest birth control just experimented in Mexico, the IUD, yes, and Bill never knew I had made that trip. I did not have any more children, and I was delighted.

Life was changing for me. I did not have money freely as I had before, Bill lost his job, and we were in a dilemma. Remember, this was Cincinnati, OH, a prejudiced town for work for black men. Bill changed, and we were not together as we were in the early days of our marriage. Finding a job was almost impossible for him, and he became despondent. We grew apart, and in 1964 my mother was moving to New York with my brother Louie, and she knew I was unhappy. She suggested I move to New York also. I jumped at the idea and told Bill to apply to a hospital in Englewood, New Jersey, his home state and the town of his birth, for medical training for a doctor. That is what he was studying when we met. He applied and was accepted, but he did

not see it through. I had exceptional vision, seeing what could be.

Hancock Singers 1954

Chapter 11
My Children

In a chapter earlier, I spoke about my babies, but they grow up and become fascinating folks. My twins, Neena and Teena, were separated in school, and I believe it was not a good idea the schools thought at the time.

Neena attended the High School of Arts and Teena went to a high school for nursing. Both were fine dancers and were in the Harlem arts school, dance troops, and other art programs. When they went to college, Teena left, and Neena was alone. Teena did not finish, but Neena decided to go to Wilberforce in Ohio to complete her education and graduated in art and dance. Teena went with Thomas, and they started a family. They married and now have three children, six grands and a newcomer on the way. My son Gary went to a predominately Jewish high school in Midwood, Brooklyn. He wanted to go to an all-Black college and chose Howard University in Washington. He graduated and met his wife Cynthia, who was also at Howard. They had three children. My son was a vice president, banker, and minister. He passed away in the year 2015 from pancreatic cancer. My daughter next to Gary, Connie, an excellent dancer, ballet and modern, she played the violin, which she studied at the Harlem School of the Arts, she went to Hofstra University and graduated, she was employed with the New York Nuclear Power company, in White Plains, NY. She has two sons and is retired.

My youngest daughter Candace attended Middlebury College in Vermont, attended Berklee Jazz music college in Boston, graduated from Brooklyn Conservatory of Music in Brooklyn. She majored in violin and minored in dance. Candy met her husband at Middlebury college; they have three children and one granddaughter. Her husband Calvin is a TV producer eleven-time Emmy award winner. Altogether I have eleven grandchildren, eight great grands, and all brands attended college. Three did not graduate, and two great grands are in college. I always ensured they participated in some art program; they heard the Harlem arts school until high school. My two older granddaughters belonged to the children's chorus at the Metropolitan operas Porgy and Bess and New City opera children's choir.

My oldest daughter said to me before going off to college when I decided that the girls should dance on a concert I was planning; "Mom, all you do is push, push, push," however, when she came home from college, she said, "Mom thanks for all you did for us." I guess my middle name is Ms. Push. I am constantly telling someone they can do it if they try. My children gave me much to sing about.

The interesting thing about seeing your children grow up and become the remarkable people they become. Neena works for a Wall Street stock firm, and she started right out of college. I worked for the company when the Opera company was on strike and suggested she apply for the job, which she did and is still with the company. Although Connie is retired now, she worked with the New York Nuclear power company when she graduated from college. Teena has three children who are grown, and her oldest daughter is an English teacher in Florida and the mother of three. Her two older children are in college. Teena's second daughter graduated from Wilberforce University and is the mother of three. She works for the State of New York as an auditor. Teena's son Mark works with his father, a legal aid.

My Children

Chapter 12

The Seamstress

Learning to sew was a gift I found in my home economics class with Ms. Scott. She was not only a teacher, but many of our teachers were. She taught nail care, how to manicure your hands.

To this day, I have not had a professional manicure because I could do my own so well. I have received compliments on my hands all my life. We first learned to make aprons and then skirts and then dresses. The class taught me to sew for myself, and as a mother with four young ladies, I saved quite a bit of money making their clothes. I even tried my hand making pants and a vest for my son when he was a toddler. When he was older, I made his vest. People saw my twins dress so lovely they asked me to sew for them. At first, I was reluctant, but I found it mentally soothing and a little lucrative. I loved feeling the fabric in my hand; when I went into a fabric shop, beautiful fabrics, my mouth would water as though it was a delicious treat. We moved to New York, I went to a job interview for simplicity patterns for a secretarial position, the interviewer looked at the suit I was wearing and asked where did I get it, I told her I made it; she then tried to recruit me for a designers position, I said, no thanks.

I had finished a business course for a stenographer, you know, typing and shorthand. I passed the government test to work as a secretary, but I knew I wanted to sing and could not allow myself to get stuck in a job permanently, so I filed with a temp agency and took only short-term jobs with corporate companies.

My doctor's nurse was going to dinner and needed a new dress. I made a green taffeta evening dress. It was pretty nice. The minister's wife heard I was making the clothes that my girls and I were wearing, decided I must make her one also, so I did. October was a busy month, and a lady from the church had beautiful pink chiffon fabric for a cocktail dress. Oh no, I said to her, I have never seen that type of fabric, she insisted; I begged her not to leave her material. She left it, I tried to make it but failed miserably; she came to pick it up on Halloween day, I must say, it was very appropriate for the day. She was shocked. I charged her anyway because I told her I could not handle that kind of fabric. On Easter, a lady arrived at my apartment, in Cincinnati, with costly fur-trimmed coal for shortening. I said to her. I do not work on coats, oh she said, the seamstress up the street told you could as she was too busy to do it for her. The lady insisted. I cut the coat a bit too short. She also was shocked. I charged her anyway.

In later years living in Brooklyn, NY, I was still sewing would make a quick dress to go dancing or o sing in at y voice teachers' annual recital. I met a teacher friend at the Head start school who was planning her wedding. She asked me to make her bridesmaid's dresses, six dresses. However, one maid decided to make her own. I did not see the ladies because they lived in Virginia, so I asked them to send me their measurements. When I arrived in Virginia, they asked who the genius made those dresses. Everyone fit perfectly, except the lady who made her own.

When I formed Classical Productions, a performing arts group, I made their gowns and costumes. When my daughter Candace married, I made all nine bridesmaids' dresses and the flower girl's dress, my little granddaughter, my son's daughter. I was still making dresses up to two hours before the wedding. My sewing machine was giving me a hard time. When my daughter Connie married, I made three bridesmaids' dresses. When my son, Gary, married, I made the bride maids' dresses for my daughter-in-law.

I designed tee shirts and sold them to workers in the Wall Street area. A friend asked me to design tee shirts for her youth organization. I developed carpal tunnel syndrome, and to this day, I still suffer from it thirty years later. I do not sew anymore. Typing does not help either.

Chapter 13

My Jobs

Outside of singing with my family and receiving compensation, my first job was babysitting for a senator, a new young senator for Charleston, WV. He called my high school and spoke to Mr. Dennis, our principal, who recommended me.

When I was called to the office, I pondered why I was being called. I didn't recall anything I could have done. I accepted the job; it was during the Christmas holidays. It was exciting. I never met the Mother. She was always on the golf course, he said. I only cared for three children, two younger ones, a baby girl about 18 months old and a four-year-old brown and blue-eyed boy. One day he was naughty, and I spanked him. When his father called to check on them, the little boy told him I spanked him; the father asked me why. I told him, and he said it gets him again if he does. The little fellow was so mad with his father for pointing me to do it again if he repeated the mischief that he ran into the hallway where there was a hope chest. He opened it and said, look, Patricia, it was his father's Klu Klux Clan Hood. He was the grand wizard. After the New Year, I could not work there again. The senator came to my house during the summer asking me to work for him. I haughtily said I am going to college and will not be doing that sort of work again. I was not just babysitting but the whole domestic routine. That summer, two White men came to speak to my Mother about being agents for a singing career in the popular field. My mother told them she would ask me. I was sitting outside by the door and could hear everything they said; I said to them again, lofty, I am going to college, no thank you. I have been approached to sing in the pop field through the years. It just was not in my heart to do so.

I asked Mother if I could go to New York, and stay with my sister for the summer, perhaps get a job before college. She allowed me to go.; but the only job I could get was a domestic position out in Long Island, a sleep-in position. That lawyer lady and husband tried to work me to death. I was so tired that night that I overslept, and when I got up, they were having breakfast and suggested I was more of a debutant and probably should look for another type of job. I said to myself, and you got that right. My brother James and his wife Lillian had a baby boy, Junior, so I babysat him for the summer. He was an adorable baby, and he loved me.

When I came home, I had a week to prepare to go to Wilberforce. It was the best school year of my life. I sang in the college choir, toured, and concerts at school. Relford Patterson was our chorus master, and he appreciated my hard work. He allowed me to teach other students, such as William Garfield Rogers's tenor. I taught him the tenor part of handle's messiah. I was the soprano soloist, and we went to Detroit, Michigan, to a huge AME church for the Christmas concert.

When I finished my freshman year at Wilberforce, my scholarship was lost because of the death of Bishop A.J. Allen, who was paying it. That summer, I worked in a neighborhood grocery store in Columbus, Oh. I had to go home to check on my situation, so I asked my cousin to work for me that weekend; I returned, and she did not work for me, and I lost my job. I had to find work to get back home, I visited a classmate who lived in the suburbs of Columbus, and the day I was there, her mother got a call for a domestic position; she could not do it, so I volunteered to take the job. It was the only job I could get.

41

I was scrubbing floors on my knees, my knees cracked and bled, I thought to myself, this is a debutant twice, on her knees. I had to make an honest dollar. Meanwhile, one of the students from WU, who was in Columbus, saw me on the street and asked me if I would sing with a band he was within Columbus. I said no, I couldn't, I did not have the heart to sing popular music.

The following jobs I held were marriage and becoming a mother until the Browns Chapel AME church in Cincinnati asked me to be their soprano soloist. I agreed with deep appreciation. I was asked to direct the junior choir. I loved that too.

When I left Cincinnati, I arrived in New York City and needed a job. The city was offering training for different jobs, so, I chose stenographer, it was the highest paying job I saw in the big blue book that I had to ask the clerk, who said to me, you don't think you are going to come in town and get a job, I said yes and why don't you look in that draw and let me look in the blue book for it. How in the world did I know there was a blue book in a drawer? I had to test for typing. I had typing at Garnet High school. It was a requirement even though I was a fine arts student. That was indeed a help. I only needed to pick up my speed to 40 words a minute. I took the six-month course and became a stenographer.

I was hired as secretary to a vice president at Montgomery Ward's department stores business building at 34th and 7th avenue in New York. I soon learned I needed to work closer to home, so I took an assistant teacher position at Union United Methodist Church when asked if I would like to work for one of the first head start programs in the country. I was there to register my youngest daughter Candace. This was perfect. It allowed me to be near my children. Because my personality overpowered the teachers, she suggested I become the music teacher, and the children loved me as I did them. As music teachers can be, I was the pied piper.

My next position was secretary to the largest Episcopal church in Brooklyn. It was a brief stay. My singing had advanced, and my teacher thought I was ready to audition. Mr. Clyde Turner, a tenor who had been on Broadway, had become a director for the Broadway Extravaganza, taking young singers across the country performing in theaters and on college campuses. He was looking for an ingénue. I seemed to fit the bill. So off I went for three months as Maria in the West Side Story and a daughter in Fiddler on the Roof. I returned, and Mrs. Hayes said the Metropolitan Opera auditioned for the extra chorus. I was shocked. I told her do you think I'm ready? I auditioned and was hired. The chorus master said that he knew a good voice when he heard one. The singers outside waiting for their turn to audition clapped when I came out.

It was an exciting time in my life, hard to believe I was working in the world's most excellent House of music. The opera I was hired for was Boris Godunov, a Russian opera, and of course, we had to learn the language of the music. I enjoyed learning the Russian lyrics. The opening opera of the season was Turandot, an Italian opera by Puccini. The chorus master decided to put me in the opera a week before the opening. There were about three of the new members added to the chorus. It was magical learning the opera and the staging so quickly. My memory skills were at their best. I was as though I was in another world when the curtain opened that night, in the far east, with an older member, Mary, leading me she left me in the crowd, and I just performed in acts I wasn't supposed to be in until I was dragged off the stage. The makeup was so natural that I could not tell my new friend for several days. To this day, Turandot is one of my favorite operas. My friend Lola a mezzo-soprano, from my voice studio, was hired at the same time as I was; we were hired to be slaves in Aida, with

Leontyne Price as Aida and Placido Domingo the tenor role. I think I said before that kneeling at Placido's feet. I saw the most beautiful feet of a man you would ever see. I was so excited and asked who he was. The answer was, "you don't know Placido Domingo? No, I did not. I didn't know anyone.

The New York City Opera company needed singers who knew the opera Turandot two years later. The Met representative recommended my name. I walked into City opera and stayed 32 years in the extra chorus. The additional choruses were best for me because I had a family to watch over and did not need to live at Lincoln Center. That's what a full-time position required, it seemed. Two years later, I auditioned for the Houston Grand Opera company for the opera Treemonisha, Kennedy Center, and Broadway. I was hired to understudy Treemonisha.

In between the opera engagements at Christmas, I worked for retail stores, some years at lord & Taylors on 5th avenue and Abraham & Strauss in downtown Brooklyn, and when I moved to Peekskill, I worked for Macy's department store. After the holiday shopping, the store managers would ask me to become a permanent clerk, oh no, the opera season was still on, and I could not tie myself up with jobs I deemed temporary.

The Met auditioned for Porgy & Bess, I was hired, and after the run, the Virginia opera company auditioned singers from the Met chorus to perform Porgy & Bess in South America. I was lucky and was away a month in several countries in SA. While in South America, a producer bought the company Living Arts company. That company gave me the lifetime dream I had in my heart, travel around the world and be paid singing. We started in Japan for three months and in Taiwan and Australia for five weeks. I was covering east to west of the country. Later we went to Hawaii, then to the United Kingdom. I was asked to go to Portugal, but the opening night at City opera was on the day to leave. I turned done the job, much to my regret later.

My operas were slowing down, and I had to work between the number of shows I was getting.

This repurchased me to sub teaching and the corporate world. The corporate world was technically getting ahead of me, so I sub-taught until I retired. I was a Christian soloist for 28 years. When I was at home, I was always singing at the church on Sunday mornings as a minister of music, and for the last twelve years, I sang and played the organ for the Christian Science Church. I loved the work. I was hired to sing with the New Jersey opera company several times, the long Island Lyric opera company often, and the Westbury opera company.

In 1984 the Metropolitan opera company decided to produce the opera, Porgy, and Bess. Arthur Mitchell, founder and director of the Dance Theater of Harlem, was on the audition board when I walked in. He asked." who is she?" the chorusmaster David Stivender said, "that's my Pat." I was poised and walked with elegance and grace. I also sang Summertime with beauty and ease. I was very sure of myself at this time of my life. I had to audition for the show because it was not the extra chorus as the main chorus. I loved the wonderful music and met so many outstanding singers.

I had just recently founded my company, Classical Productions, and asked some of the singers that I met in Porgy & Bess to work with me. Many did, and we had a great sound, the New York State Council on the Arts funded us for twenty-some years. The company performed forty-four years. The pandemic 2020 has stopped all singing and performances. Classical Production was a diverse group, several nationalities. We blended like a family. I made their gowns and costumes; I was up in the morning's wee hours, sometimes preparing costumes for the next day's concert. Sometimes I thought, I am working so hard that I am too tired to sing my solo well. I later decided to do a one-woman show. I performed it at Marble Collegiate's senior luncheon and the Black National theater. It went very well. I am looking to perform it again after the COVID-19 is over.

I would like to mention a nonprofit job as a hostess for a cable show in Peekskill, New York. I mainly interviewed artists, singers, actors. I was hostess to my production, A Classical Production. Cynthia Crayton assisted me on the show. She became the administrator for Classical productions and enabled us to receive funding from the New York State Council of the Arts for nearly twenty years.

I wanted to be a telephone operator when I finished high school, and when I went to New York for the summer, I applied for the job, but I was told they already had their quota; I learned that meant they had hired enough negros. Years later, when I moved to New York, I decided to apply again to see if I could get the job. I was hired. I said thank you, but no, thank you. I always wanted to be a travel agent, so I took a course for the position, I applied once for the job in Delaware, but they were not hiring. I also wanted to be an airline hostess, so I used and had training in New York, but when we were told we had to complete training in Florida, I decided it would get in the way of my work at the opera companies and did not go to Florida. Sometimes there are opportunities, and sometimes you wonder where they are. American Express offered me the chance to become a financial consultant, so I decided to take the training I completed except to get a license to work. It cost one thousand dollars. Of course, I did not have the monies at that time. However, I received a settlement from an automobile accident. I had the money but decided to stay in the opera world singing.

Giving up the opera was not something I could do; so, when I wasn't singing, I worked temp jobs in the corporate world or substitute teaching. I applied at Lincoln University for voice teacher and choir director but did not get the position. I felt terrible about it but eventually understood it probably was the best thing that could have happened to me at the time. I was in my seventies.

Yesterday, January 31, 2021, I prayed and asked my Heavenly Father what he wanted me to do? The next second, my telephone rang, and my friend, who has been planning a five-woman show, called to tell me she had confirmation to do the display outdoors in Delaware, and I realized I wasn't ready. I have not sung in a year. My muscles for singing are weak, and it's going to take a miracle to get the strength to do it. You better be able to answer the call when you ask God what he should have you do.

Chapter 14
Arrival In New York

I arrived in the Bronx, NY, at my brother Billie's apartment with Momma and my niece and nephew, my sister Nancy's children. My sister Nancy came to Cincinnati to pick us up. I had been waiting since May, and now it was September 1, 1964. It was good enough for me.

I had not been there a week when I got up early and went to apply for job training on a Thursday morning. My brother Billy had already trained to be a practical nurse, and I did not know what I would teach until I got to the employment office and demanded to see the book of jobs and salaries. I did not know about such a book, except my intuition said so. The clerk gave me the blue book I described, and I looked only for the highest salary. When I thought I had found a good salary, I looked to see what it was, and it was for a stenographer's position. I told the clerk this is what I wanted to train for. She signed me up, and I was on my home satisfied. I was hungry because I had not eaten all day and decided to buy some cashew nuts. When I got home, I developed a stomachache. I went to bed, and I was in severe pain the following day. Billy was on his way to the hospital to work and asked if I would like to go with him to see what was wrong. I told him yes. I was in the emergency all day; they could not draw enough blood from me to test. Billy had finished his days' work, and I was still in the room, still not able to be tested. The doctor told him to take me home and the small amount of blood they would test and maybe answer. I arrived home with him and saw my babies dirty and needing a bath from playing. I bathed all four and was starting to bathe the youngest one when the doorbell rang. It was two men in white coats with a bed from an ambulance saying, "if we don't get you to the hospital right away, you will die. I laid down on the bed, both brothers, now brother Louie and Bill off to the hospital in the ambulance. We always found something to laugh about and laughed at the hospital. The jokes were over when the nurse jammed tubs up my nose, and I was no longer conscious for three weeks. I was in an induced coma. I guess they did not tell me. When I awakened, I saw a 5-gallon jar by my bed full of green fluid from my body. What an experience I had in that coma; a spiritual world was quite noisy and busy, an old Spanish lady was next to my bed, and I could hear noises coming for her. Somehow, I would call the doctors to help her. When I was completely awake, an old Jewish lady was on the other side of my bed. Every night, the medical team would assist her in passing her bowels. One night they were helping Molly across from me. She seemed to have suffered a heart attack. The Jewish woman released her bowls, and all the patients on the ward were in misery because of the odor. I got out of my bed, got her bath bowl, went to the bathroom, filed it with water, and cleaned her up. I was accustomed to cleaning up after babies. It seemed to be the natural thing to do; however, the next day, the head nurse came to my bed and said, "I heard what you did last night. I couldn't imagine what she was talking about. She offered me a full nursing scholarship; oh no, I couldn't do that. I was going to be a stenographer.

My doctor, Dr. English, was fond of me and said I was a brilliant woman. He has never given anyone a prescription like the one he gave me; they got a divorce. They could not find a reason for my having pancreatitis, except I was depressed, and the emotional strain caused the disease. I had been hospitalized in Cincinnati for hyperglycemia.

They were not aware of it and attributed the cause of unhappiness. I never had a chance to tell them because I forgot I had the illness. I realized that I pushed so many things out of my mind and was a new person. I was looked on by many visiting doctors who asked how old she was, and they would say she was 28 years old. Oh no, she looks like a twelve-year-old. I wore a size four dress when I got out of the hospital. My mind seemed to be so alert and bright and new. I honestly was born again. One day when I was in the hospital, my husband called and threatened to bring the children and me back, that phone call caused me to drop the phone, and I started running toward an open window. I was caught by a nurse and was sedated. I believe that was the answer to Dr. English's prescription.

Everyone was at Billie's apartment a week, waiting for the completion of the apartment in Brooklyn. It was an OK lovely large three-and-a-half-bedroom apartment. It was pretty significant enough room for us all. I was so happy; I got well and started my training some months later, and by the spring, I became a stenographer. I applied for the government as all the students did when we completed our training. I was hired as a few of the other students were; however, I did not want to take on a permanent job. I had just started my voice lessons and wanted to be free to work in the music field. My first performance was with the Charles Pope choral at Carnegie Hall, not knowing exactly. I was asked to b their soloist. My new teacher, Lola Hayes, said I should wait until more training. No student of mine will represent me until I think they are ready. They were disappointed and did not know what to think.

Meanwhile, I was a secretary at Montgomery Wards' business office on Pennsylvania Ave at 34th Street. One morning, I saw my little girl Connie sitting on the steps outside the building on my way out to work one morning. It frightened me so, why wasn't she in school like the other children? Meanwhile, Candy stayed with my mother and niece when her father came to New York when her father told me that my Mother was not treating Candy like my niece. I learned of the new Early childhood center took Candy to register. She was too young, but they needed assistants for teaching, and I took the position to take Candy with me and stay near my children at home. I dropped that fancy New York office job, secretary to the vice president.

A few years went by, I was studying voice, and the teacher thought I was ready to audition for Mr. Clyde Turner to go out on the road for the Broadway Extravaganza. As Maria in the West Side Story, a daughter in Fiddler on the Roof. With prima donner soprano Lucia Hawkins, who I so admired from our studio, she was closing at Radio City Music as a soloist. I went to see her perform and went to the green room to meet her personally. I made her acquaintance and told her I looked forward to working together. After that cross-country tour, we became friends. She kept up with my career and said, you must watch some of those who come after you. They can pass you. When I was hired at the Metropolitan opera company, she did not get the opportunity to perform there, although she should have. Once I started at the Met, I was recommended to sing at New York City Opera because I knew Turandot's opera, my first opera. I walked in without an audition, and became a member. Other New York and New Jersey companies kept me remarkably busy.

I became a Christian Science Soloist, first hired by my friend Lucia to be her temporary soloist when she was on the road. Eventually, I became a full-time soloist in Brooklyn. I loved the work and spent 28 plus years as a CSC soloist.

I visited home, Charleston, WV, for our high school reunion. We were all sitting around the dining room table when the telephone rang, and it was New York calling for me to be in the Broadway show Treemonisha and be an understudy. What excitement before my family. I took off the next day with two gentlemen who were going to Philadelphia, and I went as far as Philly, and they dropped me off at the train station, and I went to New York. We went into rehearsal, and I had so much fun in the chorus I did not want to be Treemonisha. She was so dull. We opened in Washington, DC at Kennedy Center, we performed three weeks and then came into New York at the Gershwin Theater on Broadway.

When we closed at the Gershwin, the company went to the Capitol theater, and I was dropped because there was not enough room in the dressing room. I could have cared less. I was in rehearsal at the Met for Aida with Leontyne Price and did not have the time for Treemonisha anymore. The show closed after two weeks; I was paid well as if I were in the front. When the dress rehearsal for Aida was performed, I saw many members of the cast of Treemonisha trying to get in. I walked in the stage door with a smirk on my face. I knew the girls had voted me out of the Broadway show. It's hard to learn that many of those who work with don't respect their comrades. I have always loved the other singers. I guess that is why Classical Productions lasted forty-two years.

NewYork Debut Carnegie Recital Hall 1981 – Kelly Wyatt Pianist

James Randall, Photographer, Charleston,   WV State College Concert

2nd Carnegie Hall Concert Mary Ahmed, Candace Rogers, Violin, Kelly Wyatt Pianist

Chapter 15

She's Only In The Chorus

From the first time I performed on stage, it was with my family. I guessed I was accustomed to singing with a group, so I loved the chorus. Many times, I was hired to understudy I preferred the chorus. I was the lead soprano in the choir at church or in the girl's ensemble and, of course, my family. I also liked directing, as I did with the neighborhood children when my first production.

My first professional tour with the Broadway Extravaganza, with Clyde Turner, an impresario, and director. I was Maria in the West Side Story and a daughter in Fiddler On the roof. When I was hired at the Metropolitan Opera, it was for the extra chorus. I was thrilled. When I was hired at New York City opera company, I was in a different chorus. It was convenient for me, and I enjoyed singing in both opera houses. I always had enough work, and there were opera companies in Long Island and New Jersey that I worked with quite often. When the Houston Grand Opera company called, they wanted me as an understudy for the opera Treemonisha, the title role at Kennedy center and Broadway production of Scott Joplin's Treemonisha, I loved the chorus so much that when it was my time to take the position, I stayed in the chorus. It was alive and active, Treemonisha was off the stage more than on, and the chorus was always on stage.

When the Virginia opera company hired me, they offered to cover Bess and Clara for Porgy and Bess. The chorus was okay for me. The beautiful chorus music was lovely to sing. There was something special listening to a singer next to you, the harmony and just blending warmed my heart.

I performed in many solo concerts. That was showing the real me. I could communicate with the audience on my own. Paint pictures with the lyrics of the song sharing not only the beauty of the music but the story of the song. I could sense the composer's thoughts and then sell them to the audience. That is the real-time I could let go and let God. I was told to transform on stage and bring my audience with me. When I sang in Austria, the newspaper said, "she appeared in magical radiance."

The afternoon that I had my New York Debut at Carnegie Recital Hall before the name was changed to Weil Hall, I wore a red gown, not precisely the color one would wear for a debut, but it was perfect for me. My Mother was in the audience, and I often wondered how she felt. She never said anything about our singing. She just kept her pride to herself. People would say to her, Mrs. Hancock, you must be proud of your kids, she would nod and smile. Aunt Stella would speak up and say, "you ought to follow the N-word, home." Momma also came to the Met when I performed in the opening night of the opera Turandot, my very first opera.

I loved singing my solo concerts. The Amsterdam newspaper acclaimed me as A Voice of Beauty, the critic for my New York debut, written by Raoul Abdul in the Amsterdam newspaper. My coach was Mr. Kelly Wyatt, my pianist, and my daughter Candace was his page-turner. A few years later, I was again presented in concert by Velma Banks Enterprise at the recital hall. This time my daughter Candy accompanied me on the violin on some of my German Lieder Handel pieces. She was so poised and played lovely. I always worked on concert material and performed one or two a year. My hometown teachers invited me on two occasions to do a concert at West Virginia State College and, a few years later, one at the Capitol Theater in downtown Charleston. I took Candy with me, and she played for me again.

It was always a particular time to do a concert. I would go shopping for a new gown, which was exciting too. Beauty is my virtue; you must always look as lovely as you can when you are in front of an audience. People in the thirties, forties, fifties, and sixties took pride in dressing very sophisticated.

My voice teacher presented her students in concert every spring. I was on scholarship with her. I cooked and shopped for her in return for my lessons. So, I suggested that we should have a reception after the performance because everyone could refresh themselves as they mingled. I catered for the first few years until I started working at Lincoln Center, and I did not have the time. However, others took up the task and kept up the festivities. One year, I suggested to one of the singers, John miles, that we should celebrate Mrs. Hayes and we got all the other singers to be a part of it we also celebrated Jonathan Brice, our pianist, and coach. It was a grand occasion. Many African American celebrities would attend our recitals in the sixties and seventies. One year, Margaret Bonds was there, another year Shirley Verrett. I met so many great and famous artists at the time.

There was a time when I would meet and was honored to work with stars such as Leontyne Price, when I was a slave in Aida at the Met and Placido Domingo in the same opera, as I knelt at his feet and saw the most beautiful feet for a man. I did not know who he was. He was new at the company, and so was I. I met Grace Bumbry when she did her soprano role at New York City Opera, Nabucco. We also went to LA, California, at the Dorothy Pavilion Hall with Mrs. Bumbry as soprano soloist in the Opera Nabucco. There was a time when Washington, DC and LA., CA, did not have their own opera companies, and both the NYC opera and the Met traveled to present the opera to them. LA decided to build a company, and we did their opening, Carmen, the NYC opera company, did. It was the gorgeous opera house built. Now Washington has their own company as well. The opera world was so much fun and enjoyment. I was born to be in that world of music.

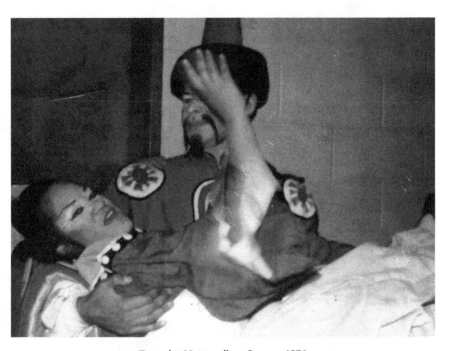

Turandot Metropolitan Opera – 1974

Madama Butterfly at Alice Tulley Hall

Nabucco New York City Opera Company

Carmen New York City Opera

Porgy and Bess Metropolitan Opera 1985-1991

Chapter 16

Negative Situations I Endured

In the music world, at the New York City Opera company when I was first hired, I remember two white fellows in the opera saying, "what's this?" one said it is salt and pepper these days.

Another fellow asked me, why don't you all get your own opera company, "good idea," I thought, so I organized Classical Productions. We have performed forty-four years and were funded by the New York State Council of the Arts for more than half that time. Some of the sopranos at the NYC opera company complained that I sang too loud. The director informed them that it was a beautiful voice. One soprano decided to elbow me to get in front of me. I assured her that she would not do that since the director placed me to lead out.

Last but not least, I endured the "Crabs in the Barrel syndrome on tour, and at the Metropolitan Opera, one of my brothers' called me a House N every night on stage during Porgy and Bess. I covered rolls such as Treemonisha, Clara, and Bess on the road, but the women never gave up. It was okay because it gave me the freedom to tour the country without worry. Being in the chorus was wonderful and worry-free. I was more interested in working than ambition to be a soloist. I learned early on to ignore negative actions from some who did not have the confidence I eluded.

Chapter 17
Great Personalities I Have Met

It's hard to know where to begin. Was it at Mrs. Hayes studio, my voice teacher? I was in the presence of many who came to her studio for our spring recital, such as Margaret bonds, pianist and composer of Negro spirituals, Nora Holt, a known Harlem radio personality, who would wave her handkerchief instead of a hand clap. Metropolitan opera star Shirley Verrett; Margaret Tynes, also a world-class soprano, lived in Italy and visited Mrs. Hayes, her voice teacher. In the second half, her professional singers would perform, Elinor Harper, Nadine Brewer, members of the Metropolitan chorus. Jonathan Brice was our pianist, and when he retired, Kelley Wyatt became our studio pianist. I introduced him to Mrs. Hayes. At the time, he was my coach. In the early days before Mr. Brice retired, he was my coach, and his studio was at Carnegie Hall.

Mrs. Hayes studio was her apartment at 1200 Fifth Avenue on the fifth floor. Marion Anderson, the world-known Contralto, had an apartment on the penthouse. The room would be filled with guests and friends spilling out into the foyer. The joy and nerves were over-flooding.

Clyde Turner, a Broadway and Met tenor, the impresario, came to her studio to audition me. I was hired on the spot as a new young singer to go on tour with him, a US tour; I never looked my age, and yes, I was unique in the business.

When I was at the Metropolitan opera house, the chorus, I met President Carter and his wife backstage. I met President Obama at a White House event some forty years later. That was the most exciting person I have ever met. I did not want to wash my hand after shaking his. Meeting Marion Anderson was early in my coming to New York. I was at Macy's department store. I rode the escalator up. When I arrived on the third floor, I saw a group of white women crowded around a very tall woman of color. I approached to see who it was, and much to my surprise, it was Marion Anderson. I stayed and waited to introduce myself to her and told her I was studying voice with Lola Hayes, and she told me she knew her and wished me luck. I would meet her in the lobby or sometimes on the street several times later. Once she asked me if I wanted to ride in her taxi with her, I declined because I took the train to Brooklyn. One day she saw me in the hallway and asked how it was going. I replied that it was slow, she said to me, "my dear, slow is sure" I have never forgotten her reply, and when I am teaching, I often remind my students of her remark.

When I was in my senior year of high school, I was backstage with Della Reese. My family group appeared at a concert with Mahalia Jackson. When Della begged me not to ruin my voice singing gospel music, I told her I was going to college. Many years later in Orange County, California, at the Chrystal Cathedral Church, Dr. Robert Schuller, the founder and pastor; whom I met some years earlier in New York for a fundraiser, Della was soloist that Sunday and I went to Rev Schuller and told him what she said to me many years ago, called on his phone to ask her to wait for me, that I was to go downstairs where she would be to tell her my story, I missed her as her limousine was leaving before she got the message. I wanted to tell her that I was in LA with the New York City opera company and had done as she suggested. Of course, when I was a teenager, I sang with Lionel Hampton's band. When he wanted to meet me, I met him many years later when I was a soloist at the 43rd Christian Science church in Harlem, New York. I snubbed him just as he had done me as a teenager—meeting Leyotyne Price at the Met Opera House when I was a slave in the opera Aida with Placido Domingo. In New York City, Beverly Sills was our boss. She had retired from her soprano career. One day, she was hungry while working at Wolf Trap, and I gave her cookies. Remember I said earlier that we would go to California in the winter and the summer to Kennedy Center or Wolf Trap.

As a little girl about nine years old I met Dinah Washing, the famous blues singer, I sang for her, and she played for me, she gave me a photographed picture, signed, "to Pat, a wonderful little girl, I love you because you love me. I remember meeting congressman Adam Clayton Powell in Washington, Dc, when we visited the house of representatives. He was imposing. Singing with the infamous soprano, Dorothy Manor, was a pleasure. She opened the Harlem School of the Arts in Harlem, and all my children attended until they graduated high school. They studied dance, art, piano, drama, violin, and clarinet. Meeting Mrs. Charles Lindbergh, wife of the infamous air pilot, while studying in Switzerland was such a pleasure. She was told by one of the singers who wanted to tarnish the reputation that I had five children, but Mrs. Lindbergh thought it was the greatest thing because she too had five children and told me so with pleasure.

Of course, working in showbusiness, one will see and meet so many artists and others in many professions.

Chapter 18
Classical Productions

I had a dream about my own company. On a trip to Washington, DC, to Kennedy center, with New York City Opera, I sat by a young white man as I chatted and thought he was listening, I realized he did not want me to sit by him, and he said to me why don't you all get your own opera company. I never get angry when someone puts a log on my fire, I later thought, good idea.

I worked and sang with groups and my family all my life, so putting a group together was simple. I invited singers I knew, and they invited singers they knew, and before you knew it, we had Classical productions. We applied for New State Funding and received funding for about 20 years. It is an elegant group, said Helen Cash Jackson, who made sure we received grants until there was no more. I loved CP more than anything, even over the world opera companies, I belonged to. It was my baby, and I loved the singers who had such respect for me and the ideas I would come up with, such as concerts, receptions, balls, the United Nations, the trip to Austria to sing with the Porgy, and Bess concert. To Charleston, WV, to perform my induction into the Hall of Fame. I was singing on the Music Barge on the river. Such romantic concerts on the barge, especially at Christmas, and the fireplace would be burning; people missed those concerts. We also loved our shows at the Italian restaurant on Fifth Avenue, a lovely room so elegant, people also miss those concerts. The crowning of the

Queen and Kings of CP, I appreciated everyone's help and the way to honor them was to choose someone to reign as Mr. CP or Ms. CP. A dream came true when we had a Military ball. We celebrated one of the oldest living Buffalo Soldiers, Dr. William Waddell. This was a dream I had had for more than thirty years. We asked the actor, Mr. Ossie Davis, to be our chairman and he did not hesitate to do so, because he too was a veteran. All military groups were invited, and the head of the New York military opened all doors for us. It was beautiful to see the guest and the army announced as the military escorted them down the red carpet.

I was asked in 2002 to be in Ms. Delaware's senior pageant for Ms. America. I was not interested; however, I gave it thought and decided to be a part of Delaware. After all, I was a Delaware artist in residence. I lived there for fifteen years. I taught school as a substitute teacher so that when opera season was in, I would be available to perform. I won the contest and went to Charleston, SC, for the main title. I won but did not win because it was down south, and that would not be the case. The audience booed and shouted, but to no avail. I could have cared less. I have always felt royal, so it was no news.

I miss the preparations, rehearsals and meeting new singers. As the resident artist, we rehearsed many years at the Christian Science retirement home. They enjoyed our concerts, and we appreciated the opportunity to perform for them. I was a Christian Science soloist for nearly thirty years and retired from regular service in 1997. However, I continued as a substitute soloist. I miss the work. It was very inspirational for my spirit.

Our rehearsal started at our apartment when I moved back to New York. I loved making lunch for the singers. I knew many of them traveled a long way to get to Brooklyn. We would chat and grow to respect one another.

Classical Productions

Chapter 19
Touring The World

My Lifelong dream was to see the world. I was living in Peekskill, NY, and had adopted a senior citizen. She was an American Indian a tough cookie. She came to me from the hospital needing a home. My family were all grown, and I was not so busy at the time, I cared for her three years, it was not easy, I was thinking of sending her to a senior nursing home when I received a phone call from the producer of the Living arts opera company saying that he would like to hire me for a world tour of Porgy and Bess, and that I should understudy Bess and Clara. I was overjoyed and my prayer was answered. During the whole tour I never performed either role. I realized that I had freedom to see the cities we were in because the soloists were not going to give up their roles. So, every morning I got up early have breakfast at a healthy food place especially the big department stores, fresh breads, fruit juice and anything else you desired.

We left New York in February and arrived in Japan, we stayed through April. Then we went to Taiwan for a week in April; We traveled to Australia and stayed from April to July, and from July to August, we were in New Zealand. Some months later we went to the United Kingdom. Ireland, England, Scotland, Wales.

I loved Japan, I found it to be my favorite country. It was so clean, the people were gracious, and quiet. I traveled alone and took the subways by myself and always felt safe. I went shopping one afternoon to buy a kimono, I bought a gorgeous pink one and have performed in it in many of my concerts. We traveled from the east to the west of Japan, riding the bullet trains, visiting the museum in Hiroshima, the town was built back so beautiful, you would never have known it had been bombed to destruction. Far north east was not so pleasant. It was cold and snowy. We were based in Tokyo, at the Hilton hotel, I had a spacious room to myself. Our performances were highly appreciated. We performed in great halls some newly built. Japan was more up to date than the US in many ways. The airport and hotels were more modern than ours at that time. I did not like the food in Japan, to this day I do not care for Japanese cuisine.

When we left Japan we went to Taiwan, the capitol Taipei. The city did not have the charm of Japan at all, its heavy traffic was frightening and trying to cross the roads were dangerous. We stayed a week and returned to New York for two weeks. We then went to Adelaide Australia. I almost died in the hotel, from bacteria fumes from the refrigerator in the room. A maid came into to clean my room and could not awaken me, I was in a very deep place. She immediately called for help, the doctor came and gave me antibiotics and throat lozenges that were a miracle in themselves. I had a rough start in Australia but had the greatest experiences in meeting people than I ever had. I met the leader of the indigenous people, through a woman who was the leader of the native people. She invited me to visit their college and I went with her and met the whole village. The leader took me to see their museum and told me the stories of the first people of the world, I believe. I met friends who would come up to me and say I looked interesting and wanted to befriend me, I wasn't afraid of any one they were all earnest and trustworthy. I met friends at church on Sundays because I always went to a Christian science Church wherever I went. People would come to me the church and invite me to see their city, I would tell them what I would like to see, such as the zoo, or to see the black swans that were indigenous to New Zealand. I chose the black swan as my personal and business logo, I always felt like a swan among the ducks in the opera company. They were always complaining about my singing. One day Lloyd Walser our chorus master at City opera told them "It's a beautiful voice'. I was ok after that until we got a new chorus master who they could manipulate. They were at it again. The sabbatical I took from City opera to go on tour was merited.

I traveled alone walking and taking the tram to see the cities, they were large very modern and alive. I was accosted once, early in the morning on my way to church, in Australia a gang of young hoodlums said to me "get out of their country" they presumed I was Asian, the parliament was in an uproar about the Asians in their country. I know, because I visited parliament to see how they were conducted and that was the argument a red head parliament person was complaining about the Asians, it was in the newspapers every day.

I met a friend at the opening night reception, and she invited me to meet the people there as she explained to me how prejudiced they were. She happened to be a Jewish artist from Long Island, New York, USA. She became a friend and asked me what I would like to see, I told her I wanted to go to the zoo. On that Sunday we were free, she picked me up at the hotel and drove to the zoo. I recall earlier talking about the wallabies, members of the Kangaroos family, they became my choir, I asked them to stand and then I directed them to sit, they responded as a crowd looked on.

On my way to New Zealand, my passport was missing, I blamed my roommate, and I could not fly with the troop. I had to remain in Australia, until I could get one from the embassy. I went back to the hotel and called my friend to let her know I had returned to in town. She immediately invited me to stay at her home.

The next day I went to her house and I had to wait two days because a plane would not be going out for two days, meanwhile, I found my passport hidden in a pocket of my suitcase. The day I left Australia, the hotel kept my luggage for me and were so kind helping me to the airport. I did not have monies, about $90 dollars, it did not dawn on me that I might have to pay my own way to New Zealand.

When I checked in with three large pieces of luggage, I carried them piggyback, hooking them together, it was easy, but the ticket agent asked for my ticket, I told her I was traveling with the group who came through two days ago; I do not know what miracle happened, but my excuse worked. I Arrived in Christ church, and was too late to perform in the opening night production. I also told our manager to change my roommate or get me a single room. The young lady I had as a roommate was the most incorrigible person I had ever encountered. A bully, and every other thing that a young lady was not. When I arrived at the hotel, I discovered that they did not change her and the next morning when I was preparing to go for breakfast, she started her little tricks, she quickly discovered that I was not to be reckoned with. One karate backhand sent her across room, breaking the TV as it hit the floor with her. I stepped over her and continued my journey to breakfast, stopping by the hotel reception desk and changing to a single room. I had to pay for the room myself, I was happy to do so, even though it took most of my weeks salary to pay for it. I was a beautiful room. I had little money that week. I went to the Christian Science church the following Sunday and sat in the rear by a little old lady with very muddy shoes. When the service was over, she asked me who I was with such a beautiful voice; I told her I was there with the Porgy and Bess company. She said she couldn't go for the opening but was planning to go, she also asked me if she could show me their city. I said I was free for the day and with my trusty nature I went with her. She took me to her estate for hot soup before venturing about the town, to my amazement she was the riches woman in Christ Church, I learned you can't judge a person just because they have on muddy shoes. We spent the day talking about the church, she said none of her family believed in her religion. Later in the evening after seeing all the sights, we happened upon a gourmet restaurant, exclusive décor sitting by a warm fireplace she said, Patricia order anything you like, I had lamb chops, my best meal of the week because I had to pay for that hotel room.

We had a reception when we went to Wellington, NZ at the ambassador of the US's home, I seemed to interest some women in conversation and was told to the director of the opera house to speak with me. She came to say hello, but it was time to go and she said she would see me at the reception after the performance. However, she was not at the reception, she let me know the next day that she fell ill at the performance and had to leave before it was over. She invited me to lunch, and I accepted we went to a seafood restaurant. I asked her if she enjoyed the show, she said not really, she said I left after I heard a beautiful voice singing the Strawberry song, of course it was me. She invited me to have dinner with her on the following Sunday and I told I would. After church, many parishioners met me and invite me to lunch, at the same time, the director arrived to pick me up, I told her I would be at the church.

We arrived in Auckland, NZ, we had lovely apartments but no heat. It was winter on the other side of the world; it did not get cold enough to have heat. We ordered heaters but to no avail, it was so chilly. I lived across the street from the museum. One day I decided to visit the museum and learned so much about the founding of NZ, that it was people from the Americas who found New Zealand.

We were invited to the native village, some of them were in the P&B company that came some years ago. We sat in on their religious service and became blood brothers, because if one is in their meetings you are then a brother. I took a picture with the woman who was the leader of the Indigenous women. She looked for me when the second group of our troop visited them, I was told.

On the following Sunday I went to the CS church and a lawyer met me and became my friend. I invited him to a concert we were doing at the theater in the afternoon, we were singing solo songs of our choice, I sang The Shepherd On The Rock, a German lieder art song with piano and clarinet accompaniment.

When I left, Wellington. My friend asked me to say hello to friends of hers in Auckland, I did and met a dear family who invited me to dinner. When I left NZ, those friends asked me to look up friends in the US, I did and discovered they lived in the same city I lived in at the time, Newark Delaware. I know now that the world is not as large as we might imagine when it comes to finding friends.

The world tour was not the first out of the country traveling, I studied in Austria, in Baden bei Wein, The Franz- Schubert Institute for poetry and performance of German Lieder songs, I studied with eighteen music instructors, language and drama. It was a summer chorus and very demanding and prejudice. I had great teachers such as Elly Ameling, and Hans Hotter, my drama coach, Madam Elizabeth Kallino, who was like our Helen Hayes of our theater in New York. I performed and the newspapers said, "she appeared in magical radiance." Another trip was to Switzerland, studying the art of French singing, in the hills of Blonay, outside of Vevey. At one our concerts I met the wife of Charles Lindberg, Ann Lindbergh, she said to me I have five children too. After a jealous singer found out I was a mother. Switzerland is beautiful, I had my own suite in the chalet that we stayed in. I could see the Matterhorn mountain from my balcony, it was snowcapped even though it was summer.

Chapter 20

Three Quarters of my Life

I have always been interested in keeping fit. From Junior high school with Mrs. Gravely our gym teacher, we learned calisthenics, toe dancing, all the way through college dance was my minor.

In 1980, not exact date, I was driving down Atlantic avenue in Brooklyn, when I noticed in my rear-view mirror, as I waited at the red light, a speeding car heading in my lane rammed me in the rear with my two granddaughters in the car with me, this was a set up accident that was quite popular in the 1980s. I started yoga practice and did it for twenty years; I stopped when I did a movement that caused my back to have terrible pain. I studied Karate a year in college. In 1987 I was t- boned in Peekskill, NY, I had physical therapy; I had swimming therapy. I had a fall going into a corporate building for job training for a bank, I did a split, causing the worst pain I had ever felt. More therapy: on the West Side highway in New York, I was T-boned again, I just continued the chiropractor treatment I started from the fall in the bank building.

In 2011 I was in a head on collision, cheated death, I heard a voice say, I had hands on and chiropractic therapy. Never stopping my chiropractic treatment weekly. I went to the gym for personal training and injured my lower back with weight lifts, continued therapy. When the insurance ran out that paid my bills, I continued paying myself. In

2013, I was exercising and dislocated my spine, the pain was so bad I had pain surgery at Bell view hospital, it went very well until the day I dropped my keys on the ground stooped over to pick them up and injured my back again needed spinal surgery, a laminectomy, at Bell view hospital, it went well; except the lower back pain returned with a vengeance. n 2015, I was T-boned in Queens NY, my fault they say; however, I beg to differ, I continued physical therapy. I went to spinal therapy in Brooklyn, NY. The COVID-19 19 has interfered with my going out for therapy, however, the NYCH TV station @ 6am has two wonderful exercise shows, one after the other, a ballerina with classical stretch, and a nurse with sit and be fit. I will forever practice staying fit.

Chapter 21

Divine Interventions

As a young girl I was hospitalized for malnutrition, I just didn't like anything but grapefruit and tomatoes, I would sit outside when I was younger and eat black dirt. I learned later my body was looking for certain minerals I yet must find out.

At the age of seven, I was born again spiritually, and was sprinkled in the African Methodist church. At thirteen, I was baptized in the river along with my sister Mary and a group from the Baptist church, I remained with the AME church.

When I was 26 years old, I was hit in the head and developed painful headaches, I was hospitalized when the doctors found a tumor on my brain the size of a golf ball. Preparation for surgery after a new set of x-rays entering the operating, the nurse said stop the tumor is not there. Through the night, I prayed and asked God to help me. He interceded.

After moving to New York from Cincinnati, I walked so much more than I had ever, I did not have proper shoes for walking and developed a bunion on my right big toe. I went to the foot doctor and he bandaged my foot and told me about a new operation for bunions; I went home and that night I prayed that I should not have the operation. When returning to the doctor a week later, he unwrapped my foot and said, Mrs. Rogers where did it go. I told him I prayed and perhaps that's what happened.

When I was 28 years old, I developed hypoglycemia, which caused pancreatitis, that caused me to be in a coma for three weeks in the hospital in the Bronx, NY.

When I awakened from the coma, I received a call at the hospital from my estranged husband who was threatening me for leaving Cincinnati and taking the children with me. I was so upset that I dropped the telephone and started running toward an open window; caught by a nurse and put to bed with a shot in the arm to put me to sleep. The next day, my Dr. said he had never given the kind of prescription that he was giving me; get a divorce. He said I was too intelligent to allow my life to be so unhappy. Five years later I filed for a divorce and my lawyer charged me $13.00 and after the judgement she sent me back the $13.00.

A few years later I realized I had not received the document, I called the lawyer and she informed me that it had not even put in the book, she informed me that she was retiring and if I had not called when I did, it would never have been recorded in the book.

I seemed to have become a newborn person, the doctors all said I had a body of a 12-year-old. I was so small when I came home, I wore a size 4 dress size. My brain seemed to excel I was doubly alive, and so grateful to God for the new me.

I started voice training and the confusion from singing with the natural voice to developing a cultivated voice, caused me to lose my voice. I developed nodes on my throat, lots of pain mentally and physically. I did not stop going to lessons, I listened to the teacher, Mrs. Lola W. Hayes, a well-known African American, who was a retired singer. She said the infamous HALL Johnson, suggested she should become a voice teacher; she was a graduate of the all-white school Radcliff college at that time; she was that fair skinned. I followed the doctor's orders, not to speak for a month, which I concurred. One day listening to an Italian art song, The violets, she was teaching me I began to sing; she rejoiced and said OH, Patricia you are singing, I retorted I thought I would stay her where I lost it until I found it again.

In 1981, in a car accident, I hit my head on the stirring wheel which caused my eyes to be in pain. So, I went to Dr. Lawrence head of the NY Eye and Ear clinic.

He did all the required test including the ink test. The prognosis was that I had Retinitis pigmentosa, for which there was no cure, and I would eventually go blind. Oh No I won't, I told him, he told me to call his assistant Dr. Chang; he confirmed his diagnosis, again, I told him I would not accept it; Dr. Chang called me crazy. I did experience the oncoming covering of the eyes, I demanded it to get out three times it tried to cover my eyes ; but I was so determined to keep my eyesight I told that devil to get out. Today I only wear low reading eyeglasses. My eye test is good, of course there is the natural aging of the eye but not to worry.

June 2011, I was sitting at a red light when an SUV came barreling through the red light and hit me head on, I heard a voice say, you know you cheated death, I just kept screaming Jesus, a knock on my window said can I help you, I am a paramedic, can I help you.

On June20, 2014, I awakened to a beautiful summer morning I tried to step out of bed, and didn't feel my legs under, I tried again and realized I was paralyzed I used two canes to get around even getting to my chiropractor and returning home assisted by a neighbor helping back into my apartment I did not even think of going to the hospital I sat for tendays. On day I was watching the evangelist Morris Cerullo who was showing a film of the late Kathryn Kullman, a known healer, who directed a young boy to get out of his wheelchair and walk; I said I'm going to stand under that same anointment and stand, I did and have been walking since that day. I have since had spinal surgery and 2019 a hip replacement. I do praise the Lord.

I prayed to God to free me free Asthma and two years ago, the new Dr. Ahmed said to me that she didn't think I had asthma but a respiratory situation that acts like asthma. We eased off lots of meds except for a few to keep me stabilized.

Since my hip replacement last year, 2019, back pain has not stopped haunting me, I have taken so many pain relief meds that do not help and only keep very sleepy. I have decided that I have 17 more years to stay awake, that I will drop all pain relievers and awaken and get something done, I was robbed of awaking brain power too long so here goes completing my writings about my life.

Just when you think there is no more to tell another miracle happens. My oldest twin daughter, Patricia Neena, became ill with the corona virus, three other women she worked with also caught it; however, they all died including the security guard on the job. I listened to my guide in my dream, who told me not to send her to the hospital, but to give her the antibiotic and steroid I had for asthma, I did and she recovered but she suffered so bad. The miracle also, is that I cared for her with lots of Lysol spray and mask and I was protected.

Notes From Admiring Friends

I have learned that we cannot see ourselves as other see us, consequently, I decided to make this chapter of letters and notes and, newspaper clippings of what others thought about me. Here are several of my favorite testimonies.

Dear Mrs. Rogers,

Your professionalism will be remembered for a long time by the United nations staff. I sincerely hope that some future occasion would afford us another opportunity, to again have the pleasure of your company at the United nations.

Bernice Wyatt's Comments

Sophistication is the word that comes to mind when I think of Patricia Rogers. She has always presented herself in a charming, self-assured manner. She sets an example of how to look the part of an artist. Not only in performance but at all times, a glow is seen when she enters a room.

This is vital when one thinks of having a career as a singer. The element of showmanship is most important. One observer referred to it as "Public Appeal".

When Patricia first came to my husband Kelly Wyatt's studio, she already had that dynamic, magical air about her. She dived into the seriousness of preparing every musical selection. So, whenever she performed on stage, she was thoroughly prepared.

Her travels took her all over the world causing countless audiences to see and experience all the aspects of her talent. Performing in numerous Operas with several companies are also a highlight of her career.

Unafraid to pursue an ideal, Patricia decided to share her musical gifts by organizing a performing group which she named "Classical productions". Fist class musicians were assembled to present programs of the highest quality. Artist performed in ensemble and as soloist. Building a program for Classical productions that an audience could love, came easy for Patricia. Her childhood and lifetime exposure to music is reflected in the wonderful presentations she has given for over forty years.

Where can I find some attractive outfits? I'll ask Patricia. She kindly directed me to a shop in Brooklyn. So, on Saturday mornings I often drove there, walking out with a smile on my face. My wardrobe had added another fashionable dress or suite that I would really enjoy wearing.

A sense of humor is always on display with Patricia. It comes as no surprise to hear about an experience and her unflappable response to comments. Remarks are not always pretty but a laugh can remove the sting. A cute story she shared took place when she was a substitute teacher. She was escorting a class down the hall at dismissal: One girl "You was a nice teacher" a boy nearby: "But she don't know nothing". What a laugh.

Patricia has experienced a wonderful musical life, filled with an enormous amount of performances and the great pleasure that performing gives to an artist.

There is more ahead. This story is not yet ended.

A Journey With Patricia H. Rogers

My journey with Patricia has a long exciting history. I can say she is real, she is vibrant, she is dedicated and committed to a world of free expression with tangible results. Words do not describe the joy and appreciation of the untold contributions made by Patricia, whether in concert halls, church gatherings, restaurant settings, or for me at the family dinner table at holiday time.

An exciting time was at the concert she performed in 1987 for my birthday celebration at Carnegie Hall in New York City. Though this was a special highlight, it was only one of the many.

Patricia is a phenomenal, sophisticated lady who for more than a decade provided the music for the annual Whitney M. Young, Jr. tributes sponsored by the World Community of Social Workers. Those concerts with Patricia and Classical productions were most rewarding as they brought sounds of a rich heritage to many people. I can say that working with Patricia and Classical productions in a variety of capacities has enriched our journey together.

This Inspirational poem by John Greenleaf "Don't Quit" can best describe the Patricia I know who has continued with me on our creative journey with music and song.

Velma D. Banks, MSW

2021

My Story Of Patricia Rogers -2-6-2021

Mrs. Rogers as I call her is sweet, kind, sassy, classy, snappy, happy and RAW! She will fight with you and stand with you whenever she has an opportunity to do so. Mrs. Rogers never stops.

So, the first time I met Patricia Rogers was at an elementary school where I was teaching and she had come to substitute for a day. We stopped to meet and greet one another while I was in hall duty and began to chat. Of course, she immediately told me she was a classically trained singer. Her charm was out of this World with her little teeny tiny self. Mrs. Rogers can charm a snake. I mean that in a good way. Her effervescent personality is every bit of lively, sparkling and high-spirited. She loves to spread joy and enthusiasm. She is highly jubilant and self-motivated.

One thing that bothered me was her traveling back and forth from New York to Delaware in all kinds of weather to do shows. I think she eventually had several car accidents and that slowed her down some.

Mrs. Rogers did a workshop at our church in Delaware based on her story and career as a classical singer combined with vocal tips. It was amazing. The beautiful gowns and archives she displayed to present her story were captivating. Then I went to see her perform several times thereafter. Her voice was immaculate.

I started taking lessons with Mrs. Rogers. I would leave work from teaching and go to her house. Most times I was so tired from those doggone children and never had one hundred percent energy, but she understood. Mrs. Rogers would work my vocal cords until she got the results she wanted. I got more confident in my singing. Remember that charm I told you about Patricia Rogers? Well, she got my cousin and I to come to one of her Classical Production performances in one of the worse snow storms New York they had in years. It was in 19? I played saxophone for the production. We weren't sure if we were going to be able to travel back to Delaware on the train because they were cancelling trips. That's how bad the weather was; not to speak of walking in that snow with those two instruments. I am not even sure what I got paid. I am sure that I cared for and loved her so much that I was willing to make that happen for her. The event was lovely, but the bad weather hindered the attendance. That's when I got to meet her children. Whew! I am so glad my cousin came with me.

When Mrs. Rogers went back to live in New York, I was somewhat relieved because she would be staying with her daughter and not be running up and down that highway. At some point she had a few physical challenges as we all do but remained poised and confident as an overcomer does. To this day she is exercising and holding her own. I would love to see her perform again. Kudos to your Patricia Rogers. You are one of a kind.

Remembering Classical Productions Ensemble

Patricia and I coached with Kelly Wyatt, studied vocally Lola Wilson Hayes, and attended Raoul Abdul and with Kelly Wyatt's German lieder Master Class.

I heard he Patricia rogers Classical Production Ensemble sing but had not thought of becoming a member until I was approached and encouraged to join by Carol Joy George, a member of the ensemble. I expressed my interest to Patricia, Ms. Rogers, and was excepted as a member.

My years with the ensemble have been enjoyable and rewarding. Performing with the ensemble, preparing solos to sing, as we all were expected to do, and occasionally traveling. Later, because of changing circumstances, we held rehearsals at Patricia's home. I called I called us the family ensemble because Patricia and her daughter, Neena, prepared dinner for us and as a family we gathered at the dinner table.

Although we are not performing at the present time, we stay connected, remembering our time together as performers and the Classical Productions Ensemble.

Audrey Miller-Sydney, Soprano

Four Daughters & Granddaughter, Debutants

Reflections Of Patricia

I think I was ten years old when I first met Patricia Handcok, my cousin from Charleston, West Virginia. She was part of a family Gospel singing group knoun as The Hancock-Washington Singers. They were on a tour managed by Pat's Aunt Stella Gore. As a part of the tour they had scheduled a concert in Washington, D.C. Needing somewhere to stay most of them stayed at home, Their must have been at least fourteen, sleeping every where including in the living room on the floor. Pat, as I call her, however in recent years she corrected me by telling me when we are in the company of others I was to call her "Pa-Tri-Cia", was what we called back in day *"The High Note"* hitter, the singer in the ensemble, when needed hit all those high notes. Louis, her younger brother was their pianist and at the age often was playing better than some grown folk. He could really play Gospel Music, As a matter of fact, he was the person who inspired me to play Gospel, until then I hated it, however I became a leading figure In Gospel Music in our city.

Many years went by and both Pat and I had grown up, and both of my parents had passed. It wasn't until then that I saw her again. She came to D.C and spent a few days in my home on East Capitol Street. By this time she had become the great singer she is, having become a member of The famous Metropolitan Opera Company in-New York and New York City Opera. Both companies she sang with for many, many years. Not only is she a great Soprano, but also a teacher and lecturer on Afro-American Music. A devoted advocate for excellence in Music, she organized and directed The Classical Productions, a company of great singers who perform Excepts from Operas, Musicals, Classical works and Nego Spirituals. I regret during her tenure with The Met I didn't get to New York to hear her, however in recent years. We have become very close and speak often by phone. She is a force not to be reasoned with, one who knows what she is doing and does it with excellence, My cousin "Pat", mean "Patricia". [smile]

Bernard C. Mavritte

Classical Productions Military Ball 2002

My Granddaughter's Notes

On this day, a diva like no other was born. I thank God for her, because she had my mom, my aunts, and uncle. Each playing vital roles in the development of the BK diva known as Tamela Dawn today. She gave me my middle name.

I thank her for all the lessons, (she was my first voice and piano teacher with her brother my uncle Louis. She told my mom to pack up my sister and I to perform opera when we were 6 and 7 l loved it by the way. She is one of the reasons I'm a teacher, she dragged me to Harlem and Manhattan to teach K-12th grade students for a couple of summers.

She said idle hands are the devils workshop, I kept my children busy so you and your sister are not exempt. The children's choir at both Lincoln Center and the Metropolitan Opera Company , trips to the museum, botanical gardens, Harlem School of the Arts, Lyndhurst, Jay Gould Mansions (she was a hostess and gave some of the most informative tours). Ferry rides,

debutante balls, long excursions in the mountains,
(I swear this lady has the energy of a million
grown toddlers and a nation on only the best
herbal diets), talked my mom into moving us to
Peekskill, (Crystal and I hated it there), but between
her saying you know the Facts of life was filmed here,
and we had no choice she knew best lol we
moved from BK.

Many were not blessed to see or experience the
83 years of walking history that I have and for
that, I am eternally grateful.

Help me wish my Nana, the classical diva who
needs no introduction but I1m giving her one
anyway, the former Ms. Delaware.
a very happy birthday.

Love you Nana Patricia Rogers

Tammy

Mrs. Rogers' Neighborhood

Imagine being invited to join the Metropolitan Opera Chorus when you are just approaching your twenty-eighth birthday. Further imagine knowing NOTHING about the City of New York and having to live and navigate in this strange new world about which you know NOTHING! What does one do? How does one even begin to approach to life in a big, strange and sometimes frightening place? There is only feasible strategy: make friends quickly!

One of the first friendly smiles I remember came from an ever-pleasant, effervescent soul named Patricia Hancock Rogers. Not only did she have a beautiful silvery voice, but a sparkling personality and a dangerously contagious laugh. Though it developed that this bubbly individual had children in my age group, no one would ever have known. Patricia had NO problem keeping up with the twenty and thirty-somethings in our chorus, and she still keeps a pace that challenges us to keep up with her.

While Patricia was at the Met, she started a singing group called "Classical Productions" and asked many of her friends and colleagues to join her in her efforts. I often tease my friend that the group name is perfect since SHE is such a class act. Some years later, Patricia gave me the great compliment of asking me to join her for some performances as well. There I learned that my friend had not only vocal skills, but the abilities in teaching, conducting, oration and choreography. Like a human sponge, my friend had clearly both absorbed and retained EVERY bit of her performance experiences from her extensive national and global travel! She was a marvel to behold.

Classical Productions performs not only operatic choruses, but sacred music, Broadway selections, and popular songs as well. Everyone involved – both performers and audience – find these concerts to celebrations of music combined with laughter and love. With the abundance of talent -- first class singers who had sung on both national and international stages – I was happy to be what Gladys Knight's Bubba termed a "doo-wopper." It was an honor just to sing with them. Patricia, however, allowed me to do some solo work and encouraged me in my efforts. Having been surrounded by artistic brilliance all my life, I was NOT accustomed to being featured. Patricia gave me the opportunity to try my wings. This her life pattern and, for this, I am truly grateful. One simply must pass on this generosity of spirit.

One of my dear friends commented after seeing me perform "Before the Parade Passes By" from HELLO, DOLLY, that the role of "Dolly" required no acting ability at all on my part. "Just put a hat and gloves on her," he said. This memory still brings a smile and a chuckle. I never would have thought of singing ANYTHING from this musical if Patricia hadn't asked me to attempt it.

It is such a pleasure for me to share just a little of my experience with my sunny, friend Patricia. She is the picture of grace, courage, faith, tenacity and fortitude. I will never forget speaking with her during the illness and ultimate transition of her only son. She actually managed to inspire me to continue in my caregiving journey with my own mother before I had to say my good-byes last January. For this, as well, I will always be grateful.

The Book of Proverbs reminds us that a thing of beauty is a joy forever. What a blessing to have friends who bring you happiness, laughter, strength and inspiration. It has been a joy to be a part of Mrs. Rogers' Neighborhood where it is ALWAYS a beautiful day!

Always,

Anita K. Taylor

Operas Performed

Metropolitan Opera

Aida

Boris Godounoff

Die Meistersinger Von Nurnberg

Cavalleria Rusticana

Otello

I Pagliacci

Turandot

Porgy and Bess

New York City Opera

Andrea Chenier

Carmen

Cinderella

Cavalleria Rusticana

Falstaff

La Rondine

Lucia di Lammermoor

Madama Butterfly

Madame Adare

I Pagliacci

Turandot

Lakmek

Le Coq D'or

Mefistofele

Miss Havisham's Fire

Nabucco

Tosca

Die Zauberflote

Houston Grand Opera

Treemonisha (Cover) Kennedy Center,Broadway

Living Arts Opera

Porgy and Bess World Tour (Cover Clara, Bess)

Long Island Lyric Opera

Faust

la Boheme

La Traviata

Madama Butterfly

Westbury State Opera

Tosca

Nabucco

Carmen

New York Grand Opera

Aida

Cavalleria Rusticana

Lucia di Lammermoor

Madama Butterfly

New Jersey State Opera

Carmen

La Giaconda

Cavalleria Rusticana

I Pagliacci

Virginia Opera

Porgy and Bess (South America)